IN THE SHADOWS OF THE TETONS

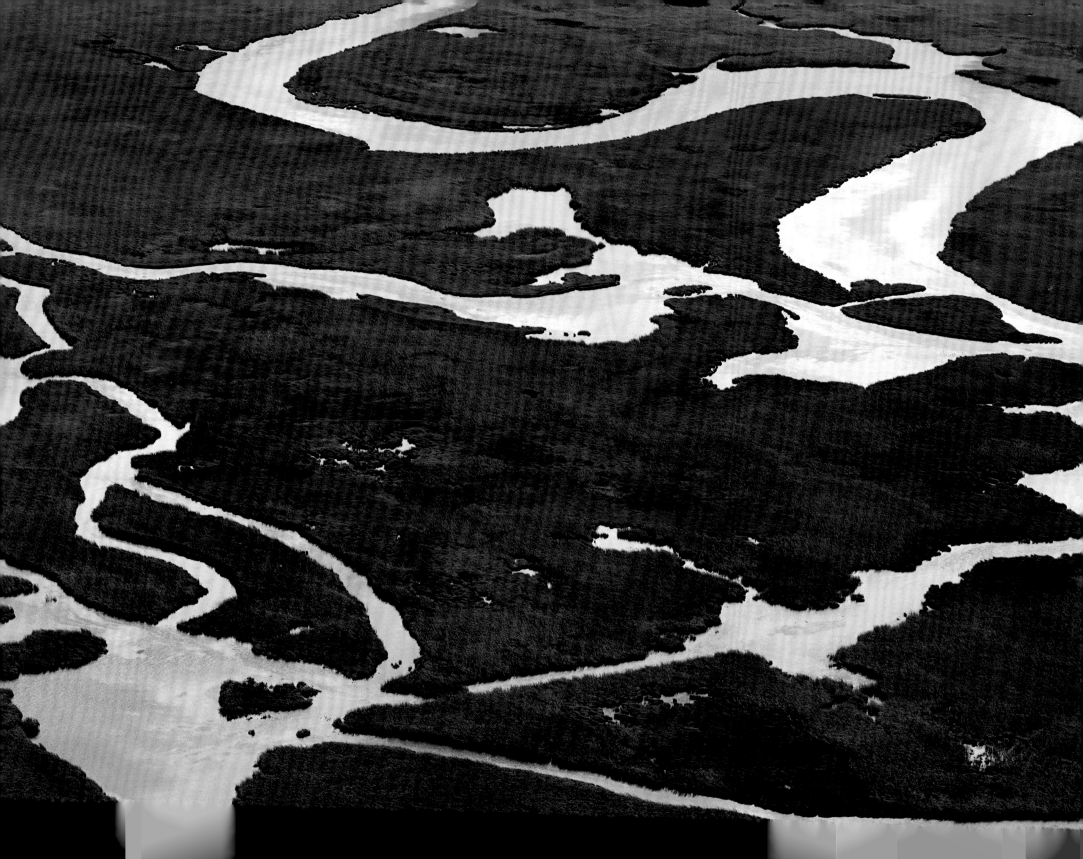

IN THE SHADOWS OF THE
TETONS
WARD + BLAKE ARCHITECTS

FOREWORD BY **DAVID BUEGE** AND **MARLON BLACKWELL**

ORO
EDITIONS

ORO Editions
Publishers of Architecture, Art, and Design

Gordon Goff: Publisher
www.oroeditions.com
info@oroeditions.com

Copyright © 2014 by ORO Editions
ISBN 978-1-941806-14-2

10 9 8 7 6 5 4 3 2 1 FIRST EDITION

Edited by
Ward+Blake Architects and ORO Editions

Book design by Pablo Mandel
www.circularstudio.com

This book as been typeset in Lyon Text,
a contemporary reading typeface for modern publications,
based on historical models of the XVI century punch cutter Robert Granjon.

Color Separations and Printing: ORO Group Ltd.
Printed in China.

This book was printed and bound using a variety of sustainable manufacturing processes and materials including, aqueous-based varnish, VOC- and formaldehyde-free glues, and phthalate-free laminations. The text is printed using offset sheetfed lithographic printing process in five color on 157gsm premium matt art paper with an off-line gloss aqueous spot varnish applied to all photographs.

ORO Editions makes a continuous effort to minimize the overall carbon footprint of its publications. As part of this goal, ORO Editions, in association with Global ReLeaf, arranges to plant trees to replace those used in the manufacturing of the paper produced for its books. Global ReLeaf is an international campaign run by American Forests, one of the world's oldest nonprofit conservation organizations. Global ReLeaf is American Forests' education and action program that helps individuals, organizations, agencies, and corporations improve the local and global environment by planting and caring for trees.

Library of Congress data available upon request.

For information on our distribution, please visit our website
www.oroeditions.com

CONTENTS

Acknowldegements

WE WOULD LIKE TO ACKNOWLEDGE the many people who have helped us through the process of creating this book. We were excited when Gordon Goff first proposed the idea to us. We have appreciated Gordon's encouragement and direction throughout the development of the book along with the creative talents of Pablo Mandel's graphic design expertise and the many other people guiding the process at ORO Publishing.

The writing is the compilation of several authors. Anne Parsons created the original project text while David J. Buege put the finishing touches on writing throughout the book as well as collaborating with Marlon Blackwell on the Foreword and Tom Ward on the Introduction. Others involved in the verbal documentation include Mitch Blake, Darla Worden, Katherine Longfield Wonson, Eliza Cross, and Katie Wilson.

Katie Wilson put in tireless hours researching the office archives for photographs, renderings, sketches, and drawings. Also, Katie Wilson, Colin Delano, Trey Terrell, Chris Jaubert, Brett Bennett, and Steve Kaness worked hard to compile, format, and develop the drawings for use in the book. In addition, we would like to thank our present and previous staff members for all of their efforts in helping us bring the projects included in this book to fruition.

Ed Riddell was gracious to allow us the use of his poetic landscape photography featured at each chapter heading with the exception of the Landes Residence landscape by Roger Wade. The Jackson Hole Historical Society provided us with the historic photos featured in the introductory pages and appendix. Our architectural photographers; Douglas Kahn, Roger Wade, Paul Warchol and J.K. Lawrence have provided us with spectacular photography throughout this book and helped us capture the essence of each project. Lyndsey Kunz provided the portrait photography of us and our staff.

Darla Worden of The Worden Group PR has been especially influential to us in the publishing of this book and continues to encourage us to pursue our passion and dedication in the search for architecture that is relevant to time and place. Our wives, Kathy Reedy and Lauralie Blake, deserve significant recognition for all of their influence, inspiration and support over the course of our partnership with their many contributions toward the success of our firm.

Most importantly, we would like to thank our many clients for their trust, patience, and generosity in allowing us to put our architectural skills to work in their behalf. They have enhanced our lives through the opportunities that they provided us and we have enjoyed the process of creating architecture in beautiful settings for some very wonderful people, who have become a special part of Ward + Blake Architects.

Western Sage

by David Buege and Marlon Blackwell

UPON CROSSING THE MISSISSIPPI RIVER west from East St. Louis on James Eads' great nineteenth-century bridge, one has met the American West at its cusp. The festivities begin in St. Louis at Eero Saarinen's Gateway Arch and the Museum of Westward Expansion, under the watchful eye of National Park Service Rangers. More Western, most Western and countless Best Westerns™ remain ahead until true Western ends somewhere in California and the Pacific Northwest, just short of Hollywood and the Pacific Coast. That the West is the most cinematic of American regions may serve to explain the fascination that it elicits from international tourists, fascination perhaps even greater than that for an average American. Europe, Asia and Australia of course have their mountains, too, but not the extensive catalog of classic films that have elevated the stature of this place of legend and mythical characters. No more monolithic than any other region, the West is a compelling cultural collage superimposed upon the great soundstage backdrop of majestic and persistent nature. If Switzerland is nearly perfect, Hollywood has convinced us that the American West is something more than that.

Jackson, Wyoming is set in the stunning, vast and varied nature of the American Cordillera, the mid-range Rockies, Jackson Hole. Sheep Mountain, the Sleeping Indian as it is also known for its illustrative profile, is the most prominent feature at the eastern edge of Jackson Hole and as mnemonic as any picture postcard. The Teton Range defines the western edge of the basin and Grand Teton is the tallest peak and the most likely feature to provoke superlatives in a place where superlatives are tough to stifle. Long meccan for adventurers, skiers and the affluent, globalization has found its way to Jackson Hole for people from many countries who know a good thing when they see it. It is a place where the space of nature and the space of architecture are antithetical, but certainly not inimical, as is demonstrated well in this monograph. Grizzlies, moose, elk and a good bottle of wine may all be found here, in close proximity. Although not all of the houses presented here are within Jackson Hole, all are no doubt informed by the sensibility that has formed there, in everything from the geology to the spirit of the place, for architects Tom Ward and Mitch Blake.

A Grand Teton view is the grail, available mostly to those who have won life's lottery; more than a few of the houses illustrated here have it. Expansive glass is a fundamental requirement, and therefore ubiquitous, but the architecture that variously frames views is just as responsible to rooms that are generous, commodious and invariably beautifully proportioned. The houses here can certainly be understood as sufficiently western to meet client expectations, especially in their scale, but there is far more to this work than the stylistic concerns and western allusions one might expect.

There are playful moments in this work, and more than a little humor, if few intimations of the western-style kitsch of Thomas C. Molesworth. It is likely that those with a taste for that find other architects, or they discover architecture's richer possibilities by working with Tom and Mitch. It is sometimes necessary to walk a fine line to satisfy exacting, sometimes idiosyncratic, clients of means with high expectations. These houses are distinctly more urbane than rustic, though some strike a balance. Most are designed for gatherings of extended families, with guesthouses to accommodate them, as families likely become even more extended in a place like this. They may serve as retreats, but one would more likely attend for the cellared wines or a billiards match than to find solitude. Home theaters and libraries make it clear that asceticism is not a consideration. And yet, for all of the comforts provided by these dwellings, nature is always close at hand and inextricably linked, and there are almost always views that range from stunning to sublime.

What is the point load of a buffalo?
I don't know; let me think. Why?
There's one on top of my house right now.

More often than not, views are the primary determinant for the forms of the houses. One need only flip quickly through these pages to understand that architects Ward + Blake configure plans to realize the maximum potential of all that each site has to offer. The first architectural gesture is quite often recorded in a simple, inarguable arc to assume the views and to honor the vivid vastness of mountains and valleys, to uphold the magnificent play of light on the white snow of mountaintops, on the mountains themselves, or on blue-green fields of western sage. If one might find that some of the projects here have certain thematic aspects in common, it also seems clear that the architects begin each project with a sense of adventure and few preconceptions aside from that of the primacy of views. The architecture is carefully crafted in response to the intricacies of challenging topographies and the limits of what each site, and owners' associations or review boards, will allow. Once the most basic parameters for the design parti have been established, rooms are configured, opportunities are discovered, and the architectural qualities are developed with great finesse. The design of what is close, including consideration of material qualities and the power of tactility and light, ensures the rewards and habitability that design at its best affords for domestic architectural space, for great rooms, and for those who are privileged to dwell within them.

On steep sites, forms cascade. On flat sites, like that of the Day residence, the articulation of volumes and shed roofs provide analogs for distant mountains. There are many allusions in the architecture presented here, layered one upon the next, from allusions to the history of western vernacular architecture to approximations of a primordial landscape, like that we see in the native plantings and the extensive water of sluices and ponds at the EHA Family house. Perhaps it is one ironic measure of the success of this meticulously constructed landscape that a passing beaver whacked one of the Aspen trees, after the photo here was taken, allowing it only a brief existence in the nature-and-architecture entry tableau of this house.

Squirrel, Idaho, is not a place one visits for the shopping. There are magnificent miles in Squirrel, in the morning shadow of Grand Teton, but here those miles are the ranchlands, farmlands and scattered patches of Fremont County forest. The views are great, of course, and the landscape austere and beautiful through the seasons. It is the setting for EarthWall II, a house that illustrates the complex ethic at the heart of the work of Ward + Blake. Constructed of the native soil using their patented post-tensioning system for rammed earth, it is materially rich and rewarding in detail, and respectful of the landscape the owners intend to farm. Other architects have used rammed earth for houses but Tom and Mitch wished to use it better.

Tom and Mitch are complementary characters. Each is a meticulous architectural craftsman. There is a sense of adventure apparent in these projects; this is more apparent the closer one studies their tectonics. If the underlying, defining sensibility in their work is local, their architectural enthusiasms are wide ranging and their influences far flung. They have a shared enthusiasm for Italy and Italian architecture, and one might see the influence of Carlo Scarpa most clearly. Elements as seemingly prosaic as the steel moment frames of some interiors, spatial and tactile as much as they are structural, have been revealed rather than hidden away. Columns in these projects transcend their structural and constructional necessity. They represent the architects' work on the tropes of architecture, variations on architectural themes from project to project in a process that suggests a game of architectural solitaire with rules and syntax approximating those of the classical orders, right down to the subtle suggestion of entasis in some. Doors receive similar special attention, especially entry doors. Weight, material, pattern and proportion are the variables addressed serially, architectural riffs akin to three chords and a hook in popular music. Arkansas architect Fay Jones suggested, in light of the acclaim for his Thorncrown Chapel, that he'd be content to make architecture limited to a simple box volume and a gable roof. The houses here suggest that Tom and Mitch haven't often been so constrained as that, but would find sufficient opportunity to make architecture within such constraints if they were.

The Red Canyon Ranch Resource Center for the Wyoming Nature Conservancy is a relatively simple building, as one might expect for this client, and as is often true for the best vernacular architecture to which this building might be compared. The program is straightforward and the space requirements are modest, but the building is replete with textural juxtapositions and a rich interplay of patterns. The red iron rock of surrounding hills and the subtle variations in the greens and browns of low vegetation are enhanced by the patination of architectural materials, especially the rust of weathering steel, conjuring painterly qualities from the sympathetic nature and culture of the setting.

The Landes House would have fit confidently in the infamous Deconstructivist Architecture exhibition (1988) at New York's Museum of Modern Art. The composition and transformed geometric figures of the floor plans recall the Prouns of Russian El Lissitzky, and are perhaps more rational than might appear when views, site conditions and patterns of use and occupation are considered.

The interior detail and material applications in Mitch's transformed Tudor house and the furniture he designed specifically for it exhibit the sort of attention to detail and material articulation that were characteristic, rhetorical Scarpa devices. Spatially, one is reminded of the rich spatial qualities of the Sea Ranch condominium that Charles Moore designed for himself, which had a similar intimacy. Tom's own house, by comparison, is more akin to a domestic cathedral, expansive and singular. Mitch's house and furniture detail may find their corollaries in the motorcycle components that Tom, a self-described gear head, designs for the 1974 Ducati he is methodically rebuilding with parts designed to be better than the original equipment they are replacing. Motivated by the pleasures of the work of making architecture and dedicated to the art, both are meticulous and inveterate makers.

INTRODUCTION

by Tom Ward and Mitch Blake

THE HOUSE WAS BUILT with a sod roof and walls of native stone on a verdant, grassy plateau somewhere on the planet. Though bemused now that neither of us remembers where it was built nor where it had been published, we'd each recognized in it some things that we knew to be significant and true. With that in our shared vision and with aspirations that we held in common, especially our enthusiasm for the possibilities for making architecture in the grit and grandeur of the Rocky Mountains and western plains, our partnership was formed. The work presented in this monograph is a representative selection of projects from the first seventeen years of that partnership and a record of the pleasures and rewards we've received through our efforts to practice and proselytize architecture in Jackson Hole.

It is a simple enough set of premises from which we work. Evaluate a site and inventory the available resources, then design a structure that honors that site and acknowledges those resources, building upon them with humility and a sense that they are incontrovertible. It isn't always so easy to do, however. Practicing architecture in an environment that is still nearly pristine places one's work in rather sharp focus and a critical perspective, as the landscape and natural environment invariably challenge the efforts of mere mortals. We have wrestled with this persistently, attempting to seize upon and utilize some of the elements that define these things and that characterize so profoundly the places in which we work.

Early in our partnership, the question was raised as to what our manifesto was to be; aren't most architects presumed to have one? The term is used advisedly, as no effort is made to catalogue or represent our work in that way. Rather, our persistent endeavor has been to understand what it was about this region, or indeed the specific conditions of any site, that is necessary for architecture with a long life, that has a sense of permanence and that accomplishes the character of the best vernacular architecture. It was obvious at once in the confluence of universal terms—the land, the site, the place—that architecture might grow in response to the characteristics of each parcel of land and all we found there as determinants that needed or deserved to be acknowledged. *Terroir*, a French term, is frequently used to describe that complex set of sensory stimuli that the specific conditions of a place impart. It is those elements of —light, climate, seasons, geology, orientation, and geographical coordinates—that provide a set of guidelines or a template for the architectural decisions we see as important. Each of those elements has innumerable subcategories and all of them inform every aspect of each of our architectural endeavors.

When asked what our sources of inspiration and influence have been, we'll readily acknowledge architectural precedents and those architects from whom we've received our greatest inspiration. Modern architects and their great work have left indelible marks on us and on our work, to be sure. Carlo Scarpa, Aldo Rossi, Tadao Ando and Le Corbusier are those architects who most often come up in our conversations. But every visual experience somehow gets catalogued and filed in the subconscious for us. Evidence of this creeps into our work, especially after our architectural pilgrimages, foreign or domestic.

Modernists can become victims of the products of modernity, or of postmodernity, and technologies can become slippery propositions if their applications aren't considered with caution. The openness and accessibility of information in the enormous quantities found in the 21st century is unprecedented, and these technologies may often prove to be distracting for practitioners of architecture. We eschew the most convoluted technical solutions, preferring clarity and simplicity, or elegance rather than unnecessary complication. The correct architectural manifestations for us express themselves using technologies that are integral, not applied, to accommodate whatever function is required from the basic tectonic components that are appropriate for the contemporary architecture that we make.

Technology has facilitated the ability to cheat in response to some of the most fundamental demands that are made upon a building as it relates to its physical location. The ease with which a space may be artificially conditioned has diminished the necessity for carefully siting a building, or for knowing and acknowledging the location of the sun at specific times of the day, month and year. There is reliance upon materials that encourage sloppy and inadequate workmanship; some techniques are more than tolerant of poor building practices which will perform adequately only until the caulking fails. Practicing at a mile above sea level does not allow such practices and once again puts a rather sharp focus on any failure.

Although we are ardent modernists, we have no reservations about drawing upon historical precedents when such quotations provide clarity to problem resolution or desirable architectural outcomes. Ancient and anonymous works have inspired us. The cliff dwellings at Chaco Canyon, the Hindu temple of Angkor Wat in Cambodia, and the small but pristine temples on the outlying Hellenic isles are amongst those that persist in memory for us. Closer to home are those aedificia in nature, the endemic geological formations found throughout our part of the continent that so often suggest things that might be applied, or implied, in an architectural context. Examples of these include Crowheart Butte in central Wyoming, the Teton Range in western Wyoming, and certainly the iconic and highly tectonic Devil's tower in northeastern Wyoming.

The series of photos that introduce each project in this book are provided as a parallel narrative that illuminates the evocative nature of the landscapes in which we live and work. They are filled with meanings and allusions, and speak to much about architecture that is for us most essential. In each of the photos there is a formal aspect like that of the composition of a painting, and like many of the qualities that we wish to be evident in the work itself.

Marcus Vitruvius' three tenets of architecture have proven to be guiding principles for millennia, and for us: firmitas, utilitas and venustas. Perhaps it is commodity, Louis Mumford's translation of utilitas that becomes most poignant here in the high mountains, given the necessity for durability and longevity in the architecture built in harsh environments. Sudden and unpredictable changes of weather, huge swings in temperature in the shoulder seasons, and the often-savage effect of the sun in high elevations must be considered as powerful determinants for architectural design. From site planning through to the final selection of materials, these environmental forces assert their presence and to ignore them is done at one's peril; they keep one humble and honest.

Many of the projects presented here could have been built a hundred years ago. The materials that many have in common have been in use for that time, and more. Ancient materials have proven themselves to be resilient, allowing them to stand the test of time. Many of the materials in our projects have been chosen to add definition to the sense of place. Some are of the place themselves—rammed earth most certainly. There can be no firmer sense of *terroir* than a structure built of that terroir.

As the planet shrinks and natural resources rapidly dwindle, sensitivity to these facts requires that we adopt a conservation ethic, especially for those of us who build upon fragile landscapes in places with harsh climates. An architecture that is responsive to cues from the land almost certainly becomes more sustainable. Architecture that utilizes materials that are suited to their task and equal to the demands of climate will necessarily diminish the consumption of materials and make fewer demands on other construction resources. The central guiding principle is defined by bioclimatic; a term that pertains here, with the implication that architecture is subservient to the demands placed upon it by location. Always, it is our desire to be appropriate to the locale, for the benefit of those who live within.

For seventeen years that now-elusive house has remained a touchstone and a recurrent trope, and we find that it comes up often in our conversations to this day. Each of us holds to values that we saw represented in the design of that house, things we've recognized as clearly important in the daily work of our collaboration and that we articulate repeatedly throughout the process of developing each new project. That elusive but archetypal house continues to inspire us, as a demonstration of a thoughtful and intentional response to the challenges of designing architecture with no ulterior motives other than the pursuit of architecture that is respectful of the locale where it is practiced, and that is appropriate and responsive to the specific requirements for each project.

THE PROJECTS

Green Knoll Residence

LOCATION Wilson, Wyoming

COMPLETION January 2012

BUILDING AREA 14,342 SQ. FT. (Main House);
6,350 SQ. FT. (Guest House); 3,002 SQ. FT. (Pool House);
987 SQ. FT. (Caretaker House)

ELEMENTS Cedar, Stone, Zinc, Sod, Steel

THE CURVILINEAR FORMS of this mountain compound for a Russian financier were designed to confirm the land's natural contours and to embrace the inherent possibilities the architects discovered in the landscape. The horizontality of the thirty-five-acre site and the surrounding low vegetation, the result of a wildfire a few years earlier, informed the structure's low-slung sod rooflines and earth-sheltered design. The 15,000-square-foot main residence and 7,000-square-foot guesthouse are tied to the dynamic of interlocking yin-yang crescents, with interior living spaces articulated by sod roofs and upturned butterfly forms along the convex datum wall of the home. The resulting low profile ties the residence to the landscape and is enhanced by the interplay of indoor and outdoor space that maximizes the natural panorama and 360-degree views.

This residential compound of house and guesthouse are supported by a caretaker's cottage and outdoor amenities that include a tennis court, basketball court, climbing wall and custom mountain bike trail. Inside there is a swimming pool, a weight room and two rooms for screening films. The architects have worked from a palette of materials—limestone, West African wenge wood, Brazilian rosewood, walnut and gold leaf—that were sourced internationally. Glass tile in the pool suggests an aquatic metaphor, enhanced by custom lighting and daylight from skylights. The pool opens to an outdoor patio and the adjoining lawn, creating a setting that is ideal for entertaining. The entire compound was fit neatly into a footprint of a mere three acres to facilitate the owner's contribution of land to a scenic easement that allows the home, and its neighbors, to sustain a remarkable and wild setting.

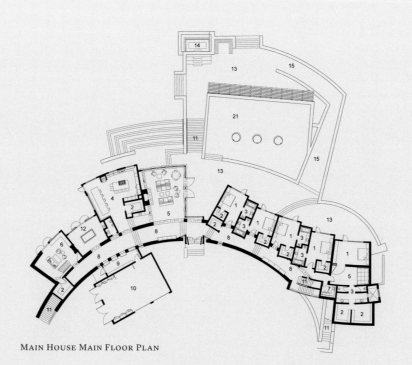

Main House Main Floor Plan

1. Bedroom
2. Closet
3. Bathroom
4. Kitchen / Dining
5. Living Room
6. Library
7. Utility
8. Gallery
9. Mud Room
10. Garage
11. Stair
12. Billards
13. Patio
14. Hot Tub
15. Ramp
16. Kid's Media Room
17. Office
18. Spa
19. Pool
20. Mechanical
21. Sod Roof
22. Gym
23. Theater

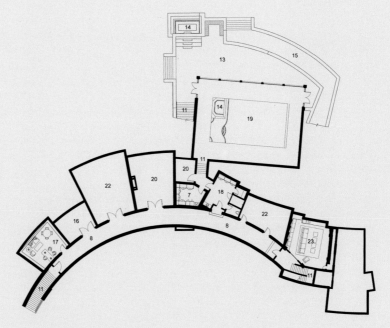

Main House Lower Floor Plan

LANDES RESIDENCE

LOCATION Jackson, Wyoming

COMPLETION October 2006

BUILDING AREA 4,913 SQ. FT.

ELEMENTS Reclaimed Fir, Steel, Concrete, Cedar

INSPIRED BY THE WILD BEAUTY of the setting, the architects wished to preserve the natural character of the land, to provide a design that is responsive to the site and sensitive to the setting. Close attention to the natural surroundings allows the house to remain nearly invisible when approached through sagebrush dotted hills. The low profile of the entrance provides only a first glimmer of the light-drenched spaces and the views soon to be discovered upon arriving through the wide, custom-designed front door. The door's pattern of repetitive vertical slots references the pattern of open slats found in a typical Western fence, a visual motif recurrent throughout the residence that also identifies a broader design theme of transparency that is found in the large glass of openings, the grated fiberglass decks that allow natural light to filter through to a daylighted basement, and the various slatted fence-like wood details—including a wall-size pocket door. The transparency thematic is also supported on a metaphorical level with the unabashed use of expressive, tactile materials including exposed concrete. The reclaimed fir flooring used throughout mediates between hard concrete and metal, with recycled snow fence incorporated as an accent for soffits and the ceiling. Sited to enhance energy efficiency as well as for views, sustainable aspects of the residence include passive solar heating, the natural insulation provided by the thermal mass of concrete walls, in-floor radiant heating, natural finishes and recycled materials. Although the aesthetic is fundamentally modernist, the home embraces Wyoming's cowboy roots with occasional playful design elements and furnishings. A breakfast bar in the kitchen features stools made of twisted rebar and antique tractor seats, horseshoes that are embedded in the concrete backsplash and the barbed wire used as an accent on the island's overhead light.

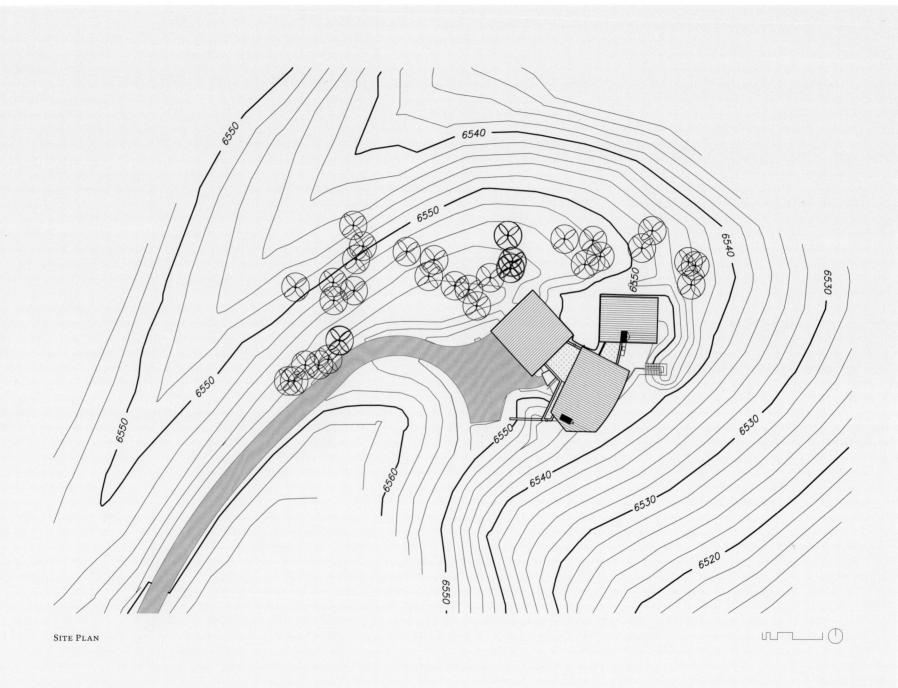

SITE PLAN

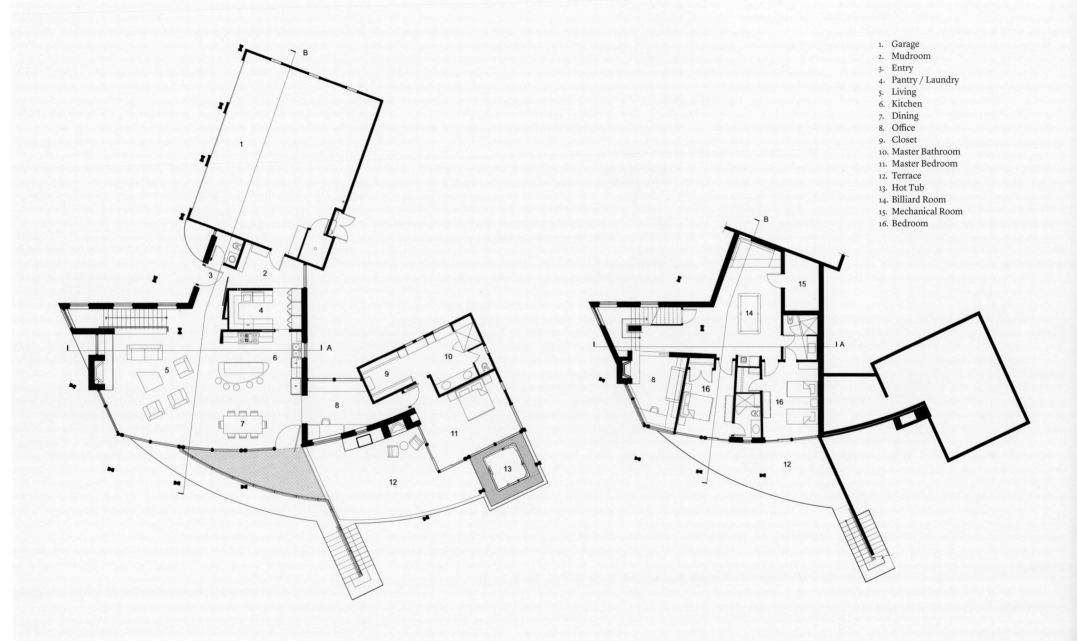

1. Garage
2. Mudroom
3. Entry
4. Pantry / Laundry
5. Living
6. Kitchen
7. Dining
8. Office
9. Closet
10. Master Bathroom
11. Master Bedroom
12. Terrace
13. Hot Tub
14. Billiard Room
15. Mechanical Room
16. Bedroom

MAIN FLOOR PLAN

LOWER FLOOR PLAN

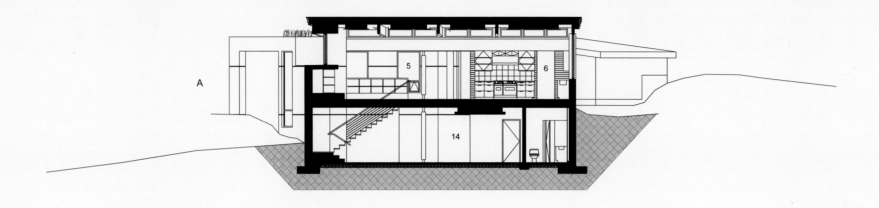

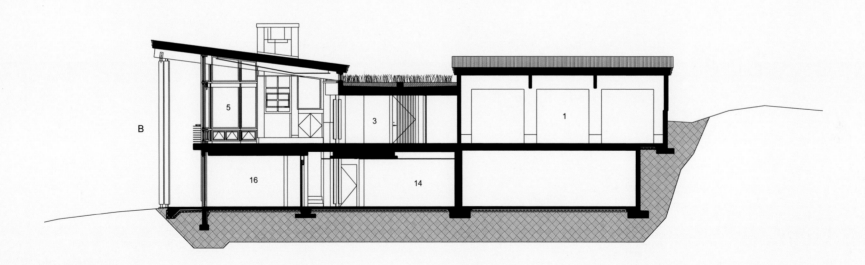

SECTIONS

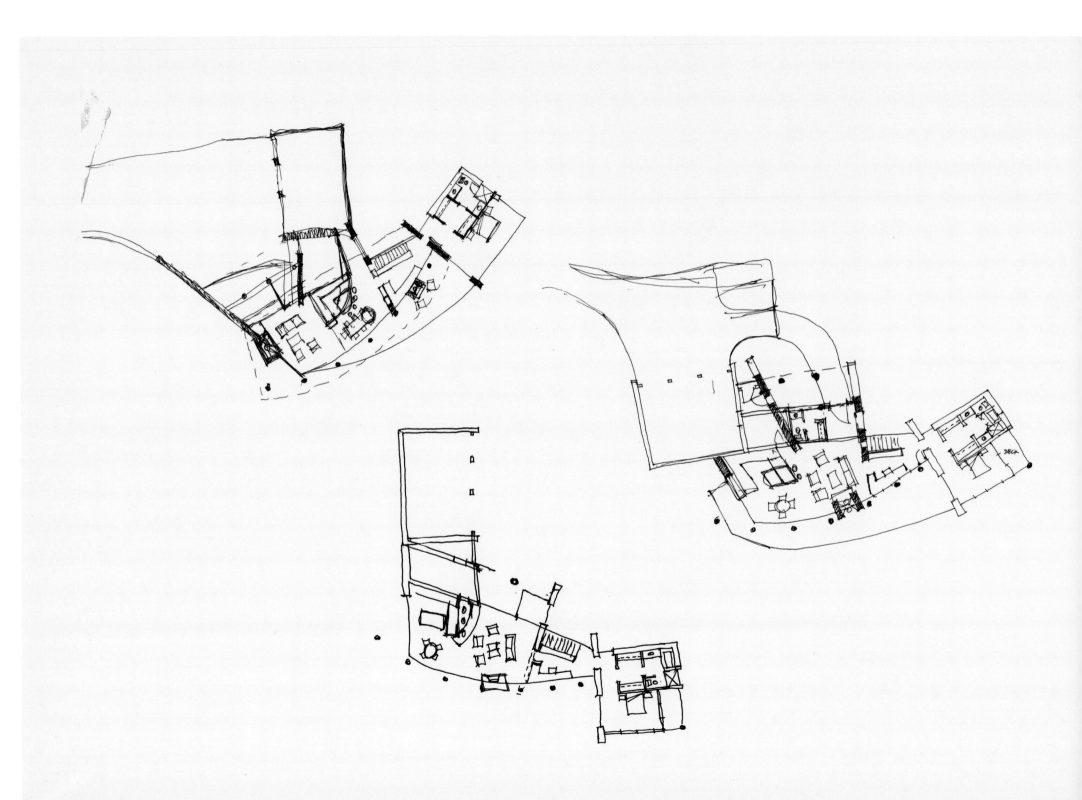

Warshaw Residence

LOCATION Jackson, Wyoming
COMPLETION December 2003
BUILDING AREA 6,000 SQ. FT.
ELEMENTS Concrete, Cedar, Marble, Water, Sod

HONORING THE NATURAL BEAUTY of the setting and responding to the intricacies of a sloped site, the Warshaw residence echelons neatly, deliberately downward from the height of its 7,000-foot crest. Cognizant of the possibility for harsh weather conditions, the residence is designed to hug the slope in plan. The sod-covered, winged rooflines and rock-colored concrete planes are angled, orienting them to deflect prevailing winds. Outdoor decks receive shade from sculptural steel trellises. Native wildflowers and grasses on flat rooftops soften the blow of arid summers, with water features designed to flow with the lines of the architecture. Water sheets from the long glass, tile and steel trough of the living room deck and is received by the channel surrounding the deck of the master bedroom. From there it pours into a reflecting pool at the level of the entrance and streams past guest rooms before settling into an infinity-edge pool on the lowest level of the house, where it reflects sky and mountains in a natural play of dynamic light and sound.

Entry to the house occurs at the natural grade, midway down the cascading plan where it marks the division between public and private spaces. A graduated series of windows in the light-filled kitchen and the living area capture views and correspond with the home's stepped-down massing. Concrete, cedar and steel constitute the material palette. Panoramic view corridors were considered paramount.

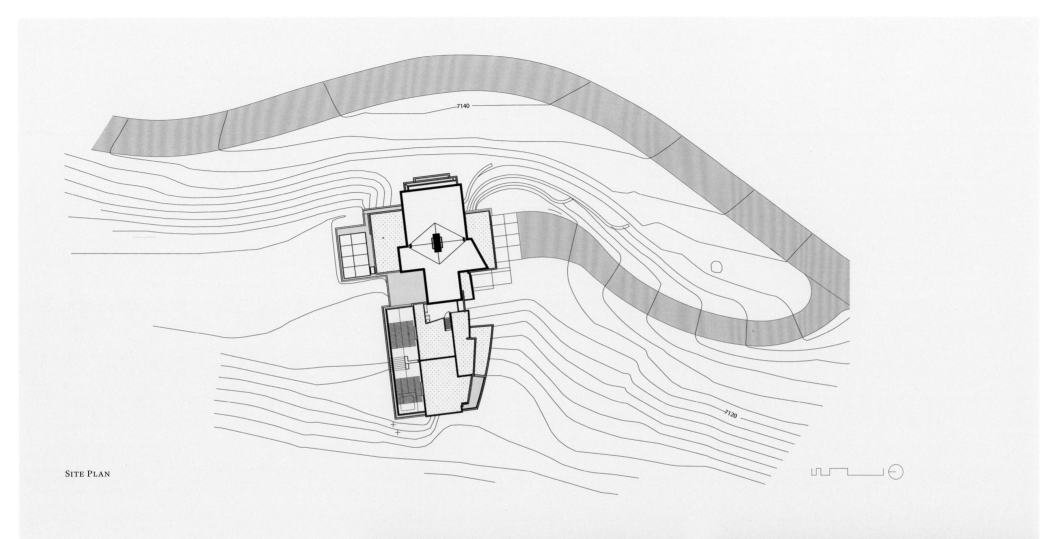

SITE PLAN

7140

7120

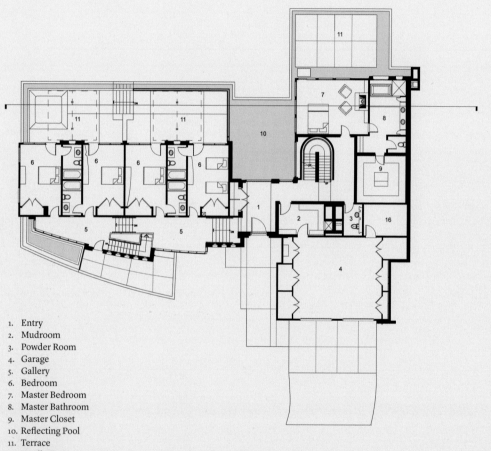

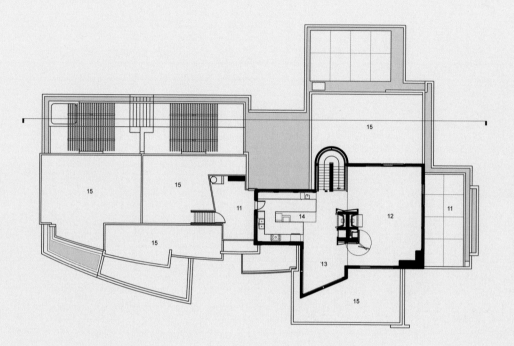

1. Entry
2. Mudroom
3. Powder Room
4. Garage
5. Gallery
6. Bedroom
7. Master Bedroom
8. Master Bathroom
9. Master Closet
10. Reflecting Pool
11. Terrace
12. Family Room
13. Dining Room
14. Kitchen
15. Sod Roof
16. Mechanical Room

MAIN FLOOR PLAN

UPPER FLOOR PLAN

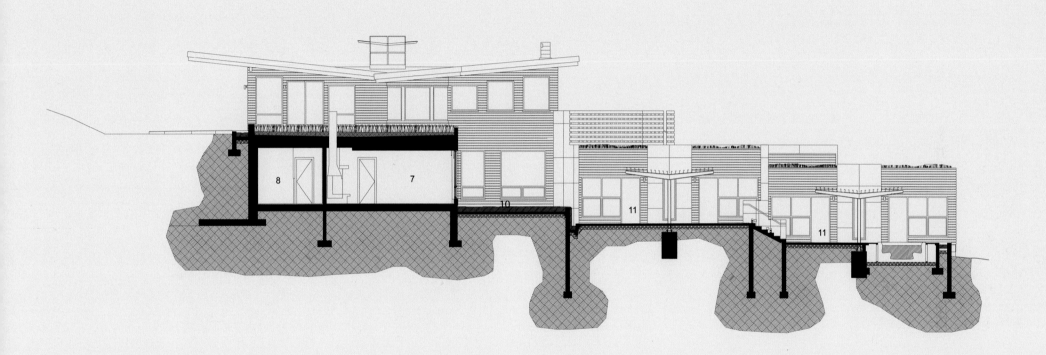

SECTION

TK Pad

LOCATION Jackson, Wyoming
COMPLETION July 2005
BUILDING AREA 3,100 SQ. FT.
ELEMENTS Earth, Glass, Steel, Concrete, Cedar

AGAINST THE BACKDROP of a reddish-brown butte ten miles south of Jackson, TK Pad is an organic element in the setting, constructed of unadorned and earthy materials. Post-tensioned, rammed earth walls using a construction system patented by the architect and used here for the first time establish a harmony between the setting and the structure. Sited to take advantage of prevailing breezes that run parallel to the hillside, the floor plan assumed a slightly flared configuration that focuses living room views on the stunning topography of sandstone bluffs to the east, an ancient remnant of an inland sea that once covered most of Wyoming. Crafted using subsoil obtained from the site, the stratified and richly colored earthen walls invite comparison of the natural world and architecture, and insight into the nature of the built environment and the essential qualities of human habitat.

Viewed in plan, the thick earth walls serve as proxy for the natural setting, creating a dynamic tension between the oblique angles of the exterior rammed earth and the interior framing that is organized to order and enhance movement through and within the open floor plan. African mahogany casework, Douglas fir ceilings and polished concrete floors with slate joints offer a rich, tactile counterpoint to the granular texture of the earth of the setting. A single gestural, structural element creates the inverted roof canopy that is formally set in opposition with the butte's downward slope, and which is fitted with internal drains that capture spring runoff for irrigation.

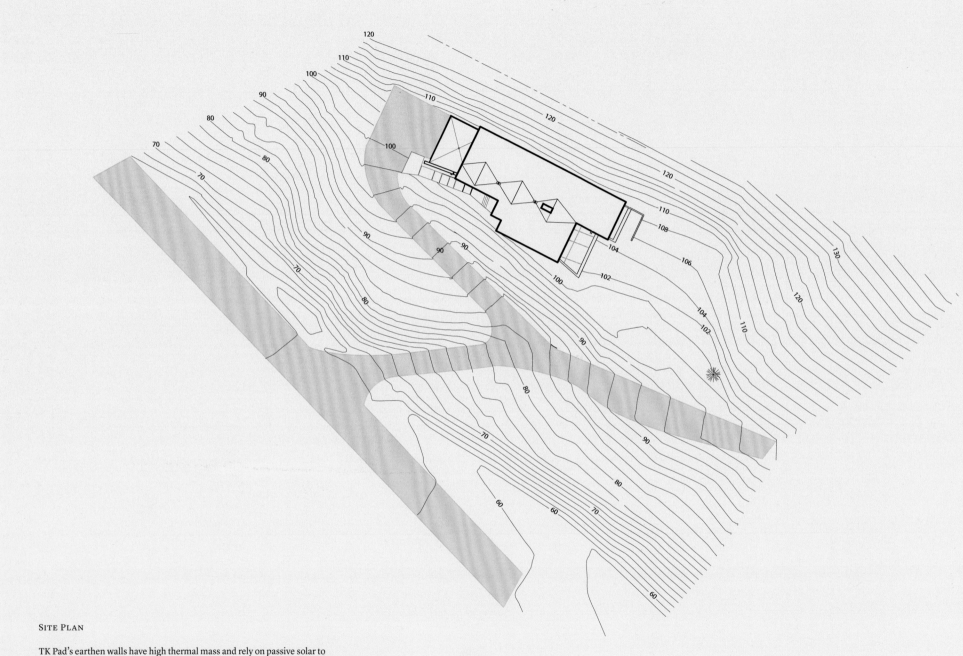

SITE PLAN

TK Pad's earthen walls have high thermal mass and rely on passive solar to
reduce energy consumption. Placing the residence on an east-west axis, architects
maximized southern exposure while capitalizing mountain views. Solarban 60
windows optimize solar gain, diffusing direct sunlight in summer and directing
energy into the house in winter.

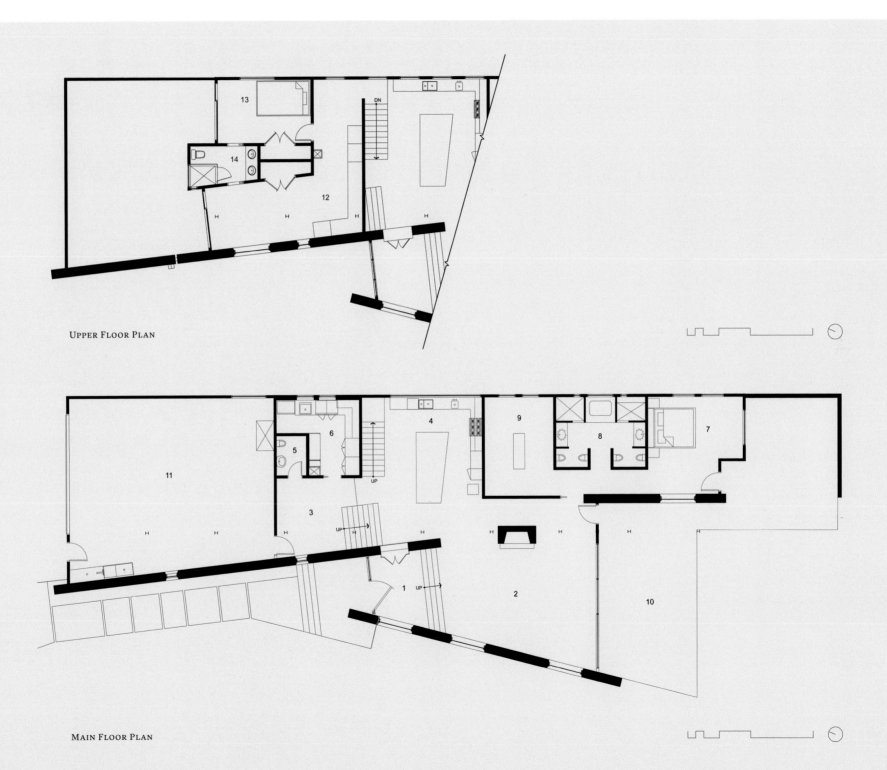

UPPER FLOOR PLAN

MAIN FLOOR PLAN

1. Entry
2. Living
3. Mudroom
4. Kitchen
5. Powder Room
6. Laundry
7. Master Bedroom
8. Master Bathroom
9. Master Closet
10. Terrace
11. Garage
12. Office
13. Bedroom
14. Bathroom

DAY RESIDENCE

LOCATION Jackson, Wyoming
COMPLETION June 2001
BUILDING AREA 7,482 SQ. FT.
ELEMENTS Log, Stone, Glass, Cedar, Copper

THE DAY RESIDENCE FLOOR PLAN is derived from a "heel-rock" arc—the fan-shaped curve of a person rocking on a heel as if turning to take in the panoramic westward view of the Snake River Range. Available from north to south without obstruction, the view unfolds as the eye moves on toward the Teton Range. Open-ended, upturned rooflines at a fourteen-degree angle serve as analogs for the sightlines of those viewing the mountain peaks. All public rooms feature Teton views to the west, with private rooms positioned on the eastern side. Both public and private spaces are accessed from a double-loaded corridor that creates a spine through the arc of the plan. Using a classic compression and release spatial composition, the home's intimate and modestly sized entrance foyer, enclosed by the stone fireplace wall, gives way to the light-filled volume of the living area that is further defined by its service as frame for floor-to-ceiling views.

The muted color palette and consistency of materials from indoors to out blurs the distinction between architectural and natural space while providing an environment of serenity from which to view the display of enveloping nature. The repeated presence of stone offers a rustic, thematic counterpoint to the refinement of a material palette that includes African mahogany woodwork, Venetian plaster walls, Indian limestone and polished Juparana granite. Lodgepole pine columns that were shaped by machine to identical diameters and then dressed by hand provide an additional play on the rustic-versus-refined theme. Carefully conceived transitions in interior finishes, the complementary colors and a range of textures from smooth to tightly burnished, enhance the resonance of magnificent views.

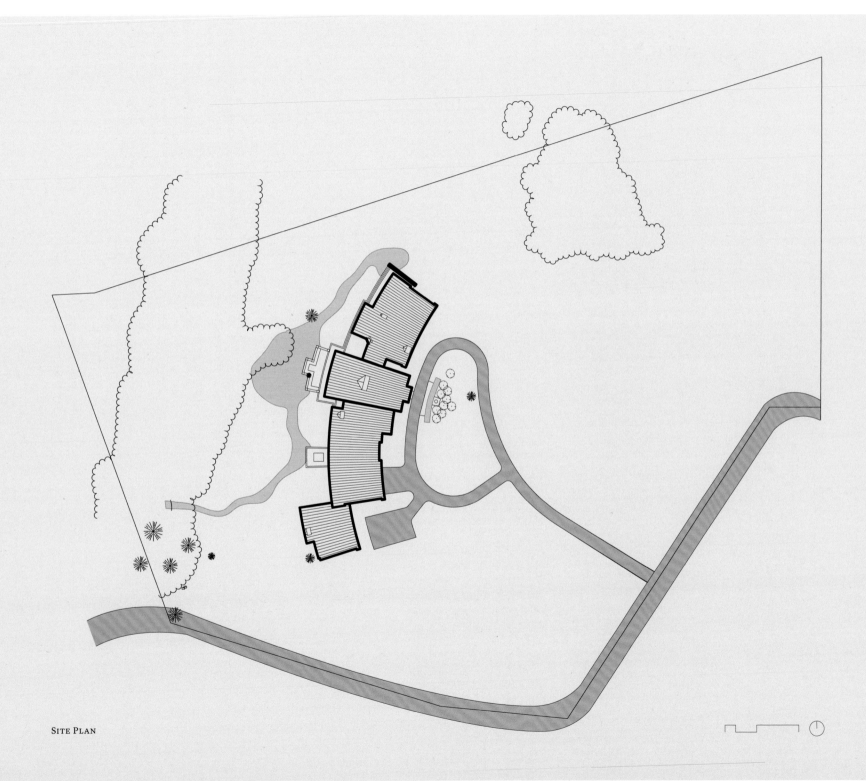

SITE PLAN

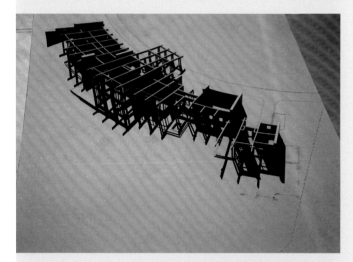

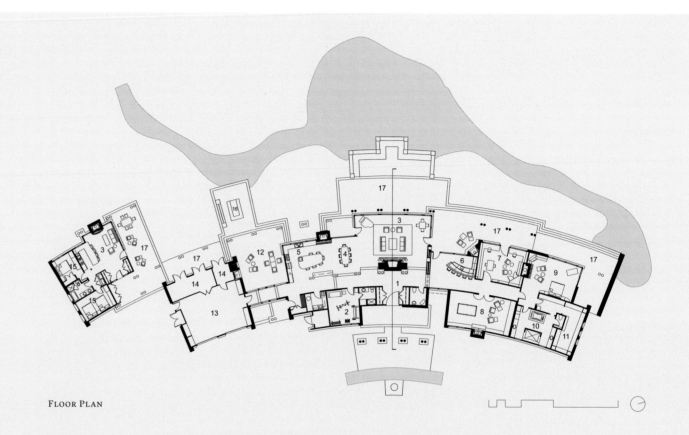

FLOOR PLAN

1. Entry
2. Exercise Room
3. Living
4. Dining
5. Kitchen
6. Bar
7. Library
8. Media / Game Room
9. Master Bedroom
10. Master Bathroom
11. Master Closet
12. Bar-B-Que Patio
13. Garage
14. Storage
15. Bedroom
16. Hot Tub
17. Terrace

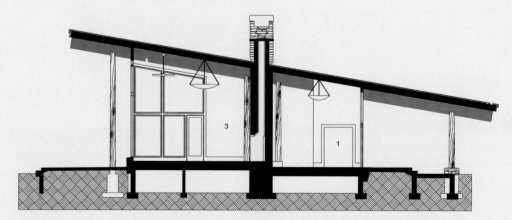

SECTION

VILLA DI FAMIGLIA VITA

LOCATION Alta, Wyoming
COMPLETION October 2011
BUILDING AREA 4,452 SQ. FT.
ELEMENTS Corten, Cem-Clad Panels, Mild Steel, Cedar, Sod

T HIS EXTENSIVE RENOVATION of a 1980s Tudor-style residence builds upon the original structure's solid bones and characteristic formal composition, and an excellent site orientation, while substantially refashioning it with a modernist design sensibility suited to the needs of a large, active family. A four-foot extension was made to the existing kitchen and porch, a new roofline was created to accommodate a restructured guest bedroom and the space of the original porte-cochere was reintroduced, transforming the look of the home and giving it new life. The unfinished attic was converted as a children's floor with dual bunkrooms, a playroom and an open media room, creating a much-beloved space that is appropriately scaled for young users.

Despite what might be suggested by an imposing façade, the Villa integrates sustainable construction techniques, systems and materials. Corten steel, Cem-Clad panels, steel and cedar, provide thematic continuity from exterior to interior spaces with the benefit of low-maintenance requirements. Enlargement of existing windows and the addition of new windows further opened the interior to the natural surroundings and enhanced the availability of natural light. Sod roofs were added where possible to ease the connection of the outdoor environment with interior spaces, and to reduce temperature fluctuations for improved energy efficiency.

The new and most prominent element of the interior, a glass and steel staircase, winds through all three levels, an irregular zigzag in form that is accentuated by its transparent quality. Douglas-fir ceiling panels, bamboo floors, numerous built-ins, ponderosa pine-clad windows and furniture designed by the architect provide warmth, personality and a sense of intimacy in previously conventional interior spaces. The eighty-five-percent renovation of this formerly unremarkable structure brings an architectural vision to a dynamic family's requirements for a modern reimagining of home.

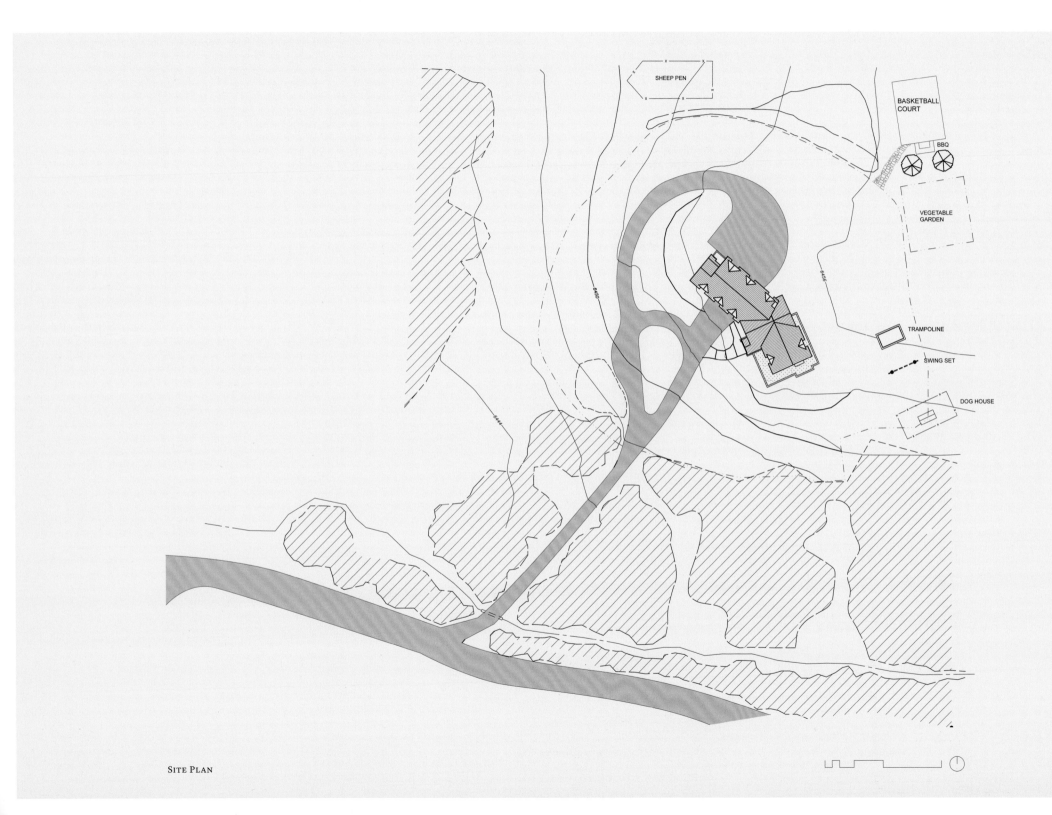

SHEEP PEN

BASKETBALL
COURT

BBQ

VEGETABLE
GARDEN

TRAMPOLINE

SWING SET

DOG HOUSE

SITE PLAN

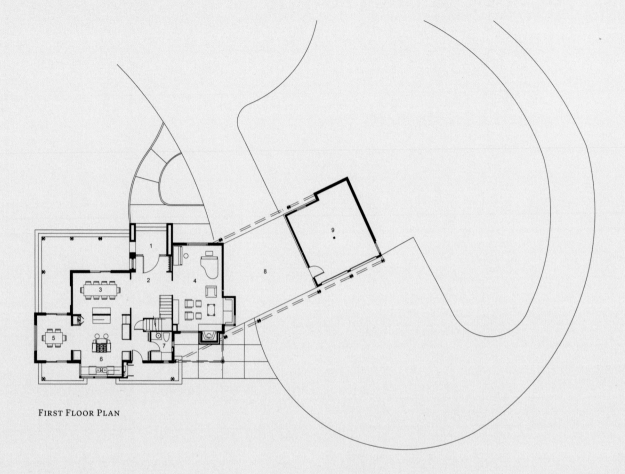

FIRST FLOOR PLAN

1.   Entry Porch
2.   Entry
3.   Dining
4.   Living Room
5.   Breakfast
6.   Kitchen
7.   Powder Room
8.   Car Port
9.   Garage
10. Bedroom
11. Bathroom
12. Library
13. Office
14. Workout Room
15. Closet
16. Master Bedroom
17. Master Bathroom
18. Master Closet
19. Laundry
20. Mechanical Room
21. Sod Roof
22. Play Room
23. Play Cubbie
24. Bunk Room
25. Bridge
26. Storage
27. Media Room

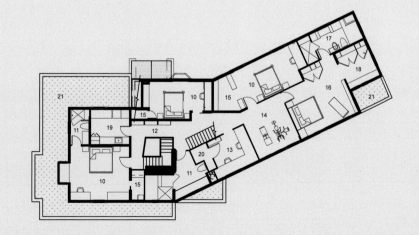

SECOND FLOOR PLAN

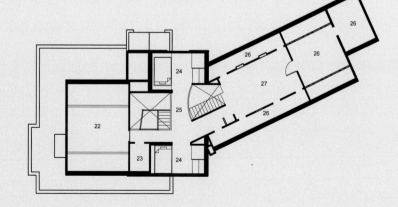

ATTIC FLOOR PLAN

Commercial, Institutional & Unbuilt Residences

SPRING CREEK RANCH

LOCATION Jackson, Wyoming
COMPLETION August 2002
BUILDING AREA 18,116 SQ. FT.
ELEMENTS Cedar, Stained Concrete, Rusted Steel, Painted Steel, Natural Log

DRAWING UPON THE DUDE RANCH LODGES and "auto camp" reception facilities that have peppered Jackson Hole for nearly a century, the architects have brought new life to the building type established by these vernacular precedents in their design for the headquarters building at the Spring Creek Ranch. The multi-faceted program is comprised of a reception area, offices, spa facilities, a salon and a convention center, collected in a single long and narrow building envelope that is organized along an east-west axis. Outdoor terraces provide guests with opportunities to relax and to take in the magnificence of the setting. Building form and orientation are guided by county height and skyline restrictions, as well as by a desire to optimize views of the Teton Range. Clear and direct in form, the plan's long, narrow layout is enhanced by an exposed structure and architectural details that augment the building's simple form.

Exposed steel columns are partially clad by split logs that support bull hide-covered laminated wood beams. Acid-stained concrete floors complement the columns and beams. Together, this contemporary application of these materials conveys subtle, Old West regional allusions.

The low-pitched rooflines are those that originated with regional ranch precedents, but these deviate from established stylistic norms by extending significantly beyond the vertical walls, where they are received by exposed steel supports that rise toward the roof at an oblique angle. Similarly, exposed structural elements featured on the interior—such as wood-wrapped steel columns and hanging steel wires that literally hold the fireplace mantel in place—call attention to the spatial character of the structure. The combination of an exposed structure and the use of natural, significant local materials characterize this no-nonsense building, beginning at the entry that is designed to receive and immediately engage approaching guests.

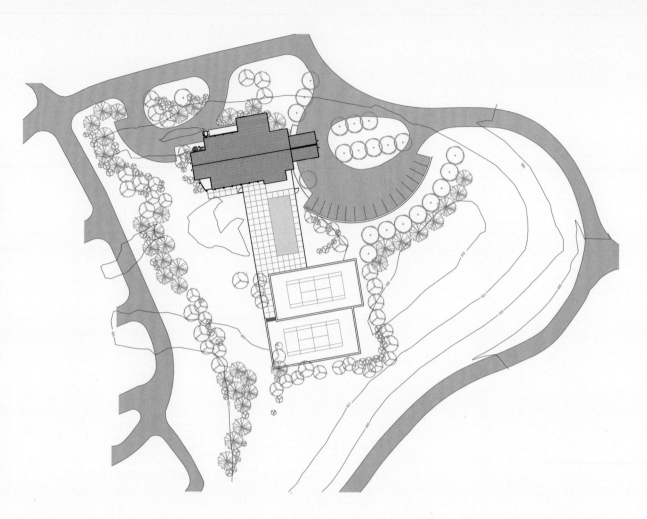

SITE PLAN

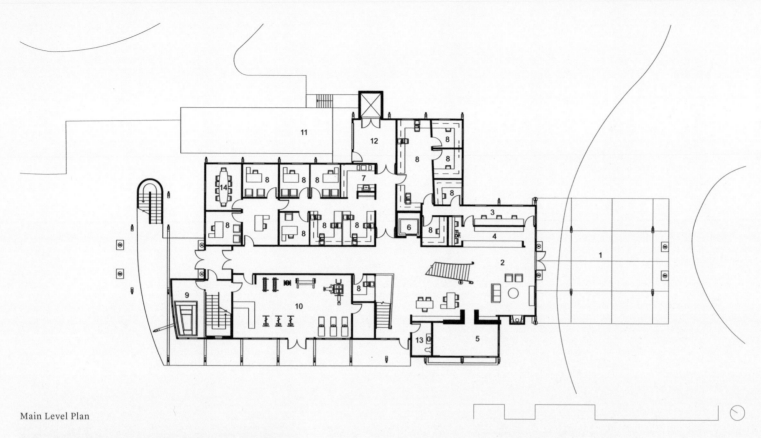

1. Porte Cochere
2. Lobby
3. Reservations
4. Front Desk
5. Gift Shop
6. Elevator
7. Kitchen
8. Office
9. Hot Tub
10. Workout Room
11. Loading Dock
12. Staging
13. Restroom
14. Conference Room

Main Level Plan

WYOMING NATURE CONSERVANCY

LOCATION Lander, Wyoming
COMPLETION June 1998
BUILDING AREA 2,079 SQ. FT. Enclosed; 1,878 SQ. FT. Patio
ELEMENTS Rammed Earth, Native Log, Weathered Steel, Concrete, Glass

LOCATED ON A 5,000-ACRE working cow and calf ranch in south central Wyoming's biologically and archaeologically significant Red Canyon, the Nature Conservancy's Red Canyon Ranch Resource Center serves both as a living classroom for contemporary seekers in the environmentally critical area of conservation grazing practices, and as a "stop along the way" on an ancient trail that has been frequented by humans for more than 10,000 years. Once traveled by Folsom tribal hunters, this path is expressed symbolically in architectural details and in analogous, exposed aggregate concrete floors. The iron-rich Triassic soil that provides the vivid color of the canyon becomes a literal part of the building, whose walls are constructed primarily of locally sourced rammed-earth. Non-galvanized corrugated steel roof panels and treillage, weathered native log support columns and tubular steel further integrate the building into its panoramic canyon setting, enhancing an already compelling sense of place.

The application of low-impact technology underscores the Red Canyon Ranch's environmental mission. Thermal mass provided by the rammed earth walls minimizes the heating and cooling requirements for the building and diminish overall carbon emissions while reducing construction waste as well. Additional sustainable features include waterless composting toilets, a wastewater disposal system that allows grey water to be used for irrigation, and compact fluorescent and indirect halogen fixtures for lighting. Tubing within the concrete floors distributes radiant heat supplied by a high-efficiency, wood-fired boiler and stove with two-stage combustion, designed in Wyoming, that virtually eliminates air pollution.

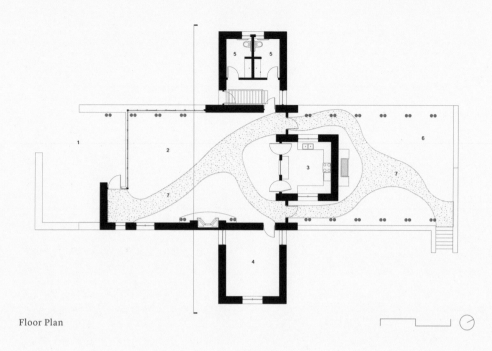

Floor Plan

Section

1. Entry Patio
2. Meeting Room
3. Kitchen
4. Office
5. Bathroom
6. Outdoor Patio
7. Trail

TETON COUNTY CHILDREN'S LEARNING CENTER, "THE RANCH"

LOCATION Jackson, Wyoming
COMPLETION January 2011
BUILDING AREA 12,000 SQ. FT.
ELEMENTS Rammed Earth, Cedar, Glass, Steel, Sod Roof, Weathered Wood

WARD + BLAKE COLLABORATED with D. W. Arthur Associates, early childhood education design specialists, in the kid-focused design process for the Teton County Children's Learning Center, popularly known as "The Ranch." The endeavor was to create the setting for a new sort of dialogue between pre-literate children, architecture and the natural world. As a careful addition to its remarkable Jackson Hole wetlands setting, the architecture serves as a teaching tool in its own right. Using a "family-room" concept with gently curving, embracing walls defining spaces in which children of different ages interact within the broader community, the building's primary corridor opens to private rooms that serve specific needs and ages. Glass expanses and clerestory windows receive natural light. A rooftop play space extends and brings clarity to the continuity between indoor and outdoor space.

In the surrounding landscape, where they may follow wildlife tracks along a Snake River tributary, preschoolers learn to walk lightly in the fragile habitat of a complex wetlands ecosystem that is located within the migratory path for Trumpeter swans. Remaining circumspect and respectful of the surrounding residential neighborhood, the exterior of the 12,000-square-foot building is carefully resolved into smaller masses that reference such iconic regional motifs as beaver slides, horizontally slatted fence lines, and the evolution of the typical ranch outbuildings of the region.

Sustainability is an important aspect of the Learning Center mission. Supporting that mission, the architecture incorporates a closed loop ground source heat pump that offers geothermal heating and cooling without impacting natural water sources, adding major points in the certification process that ultimately granted a LEED Gold rating. A smart heating and lighting system adjusts automatically to ensure greatest efficiency, diminishing energy required by half that of other county buildings. The Learning Center consumes less than half the water than that of an average childcare center.

SITE PLAN

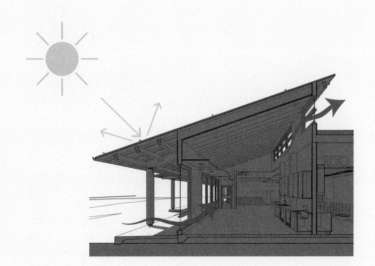

NORTH ELEVATION

WEST ELEVATION

PLC RESIDENCE

LOCATION Jackson, Wyoming
COMPLETION Unbuilt
BUILDING AREA 8,105 SQ. FT.
ELEMENTS Rammed Earth, Cedar, Glass, Concrete, Sod

THE ELONGATED C-SHAPE OF A FRENCH CURVE, evident in the earliest hand sketches from the design process, orients this Jackson Hole residence to maximize views across the 300-degree butte-top panorama. This curve is repeated as a freestanding, rammed earth exterior wall that provides privacy from a road passing above the site. Cut into the site's gradient to create a descending and dramatic drive-in entrance, the house features expansive areas of glass commanding the most impressive views, with the transparency of the upper-level pavilions complemented by the solidity of earthen walls for the lower level, crafted with post-tensioned rammed earth for seismic stability. An arching hallway joins programmatically distinct masses to serve as the principal organizing device for the residence's spatial geometry. Sod roof decks, terraces, water features and patios create multiple outdoor living rooms, bringing together elements of the built and natural environments.

The thermal mass of rammed earth and concrete floors offsets heat loss due to the preponderant glazing of upper levels. Large roof overhangs allow passive solar heat gain in winter while helping to shade the triple-pane high-efficiency glazing in summer. Additional green environmental principles are represented by stepped sod roofs, heat delivered hydronically by tubing in the concrete floors, water features that temper the arid Wyoming climate, and a closed-loop ground source heat pump and back-up natural gas boiler for heating and cooling. Energy recovery generators keep the interior air-conditioned and operable windows facilitate cross-ventilation to capture natural breezes.

WEST ELEVATION

1. Entry Drive
2. Entry
3. Garage
4. Mechanical Room
5. Mudroom
6. Laundry
7. Stair Lobby
8. Bar
9. Billiard
10. Media
11. Powder Room
12. Reflecting Pool
13. Bedroom
14. Office
15. Gallery
16. Fitness
17. Sauna
18. Bunk Room
19. Terrace
20. Hot Tub
21. Master Bedroom
22. Master Bathroom
23. Master Closet
24. Living Room
25. Dining Room
26. Kitchen
27. Sod Roof
28. Lap Pool

MAIN FLOOR PLAN

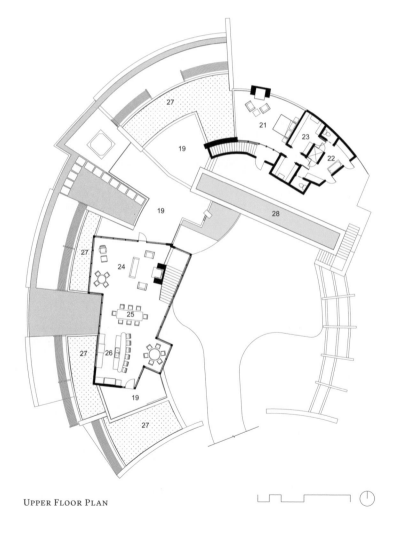

UPPER FLOOR PLAN

THREE CREEK RESIDENCE

LOCATION Jackson, Wyoming
COMPLETION Unbuilt
BUILDING AREA 10,300 SQ. FT.
ELEMENTS Stone, Corten, Cedar, Steel, Mahogany

A LOW PROFILE HAS BEEN PROVIDED in response to the site's flat topography, allowing the Three Creek Residence to capture both short and distant mountain views while diminishing the house's apparent mass and the possibility that it might dominate the immediate setting. A seemingly contradictory requirement was to provide guest quarters above a stand-alone garage, which was resolved by setting the garage one full level below the existing grade.

The main level of the residence, including the living room, is set two feet below the existing grade, and with shallow roof pitches the apparent building mass is reduced. An exterior material palette that includes native stone, repurposed lumber siding and iron roofing further enhances this visual reticence and formal integration of the structure into its natural setting. Exterior walls are treated as planes that peel away. The expanses of glass are designed to control glare while providing light and vignette views for the most significant interior spaces. A long east-west hallway, top-lit with northern light via clerestory windows, organizes circulation for private areas of the residence and provides gallery space for the display of a large collection of contemporary art.

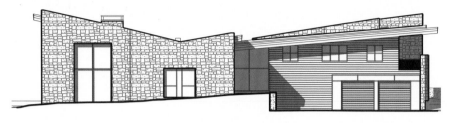

WEST ELEVATION

NORTH ELEVATION

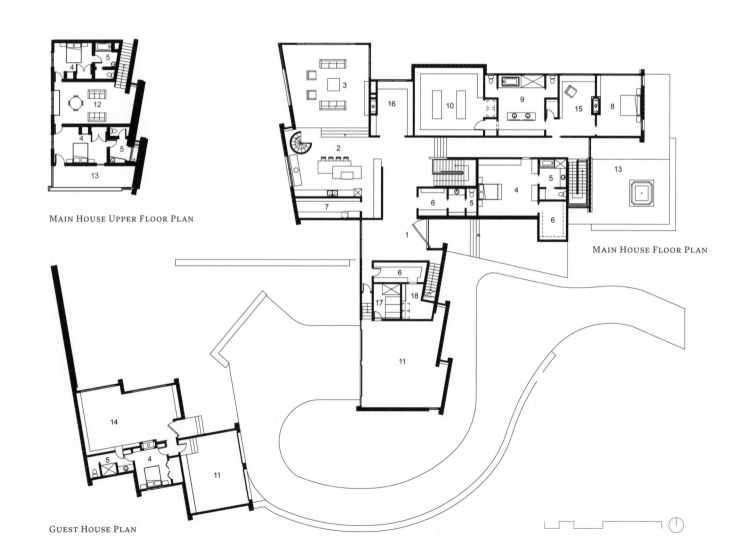

MAIN HOUSE UPPER FLOOR PLAN

MAIN HOUSE FLOOR PLAN

GUEST HOUSE PLAN

1. Entry
2. Kitchen
3. Living
4. Bedroom
5. Bathroom
6. Closet
7. Pantry
8. Master Bedroom
9. Master Bathroom
10. Master Closet
11. Garage
12. Common Room
13. Patio
14. Office
15. Sitting Room
16. Library
17. Dog Wash
18. Laundry

SHARP RESIDENCE

LOCATION Freedom, Wyoming
COMPLETION Unbuilt
BUILDING AREA 3,600 SQ. FT.
ELEMENTS Concrete, Glass Block, Cedar, Steel

LOCATED ON THE UPPER SLOPES of pastureland overlooking a family farm in rural western Wyoming, with distant mountain vistas and nestled against a dense stand of trees, the earth-sheltered design of the Sharp residence creates a line of engagement with nature by its smooth integration into the grassy sloped site. The driveway arrives at the garage on the uphill side offering unencumbered views downslope. The daylighted basement has two walkout apertures that allow the main level of the residence to engage the slope.

The elements of the open plan include a spacious kitchen, living room, library, media room, exercise room, racquetball court, five bedrooms and five and a half bathrooms. Glass blocks set into the floor of the main level deliver natural light to the basement hallway. The low-impact design of the house, important to its situation on the land of an operating farm, also includes such energy-conscious features as concrete walls for thermal mass and a ground source heat pump. Excavated fill from the basement was utilized to enhance an existing stream by the creation of three small ponds.

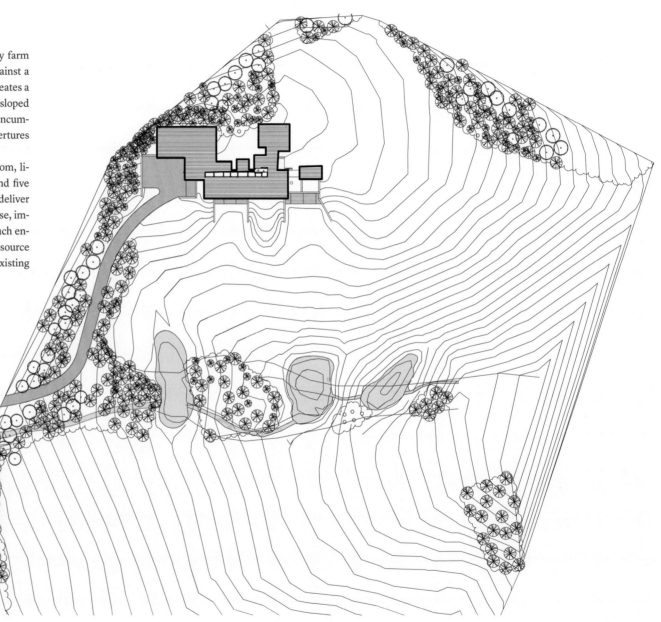

Site Plan

NORTH ELEVATION

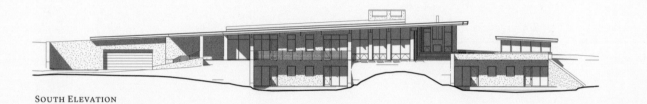

SOUTH ELEVATION

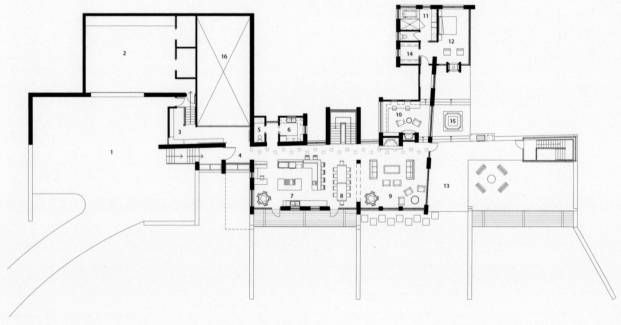

MAIN FLOOR PLAN

1. Entry Court
2. Garage
3. Mud Room
4. Entry
5. Powder
6. Laundry
7. Kitchen
8. Dining
9. Living
10. Library
11. Master Bath
12. Master Bed
13. Terrace
14. Closet
15. Hot Tub
16. Raquetball Court

SPLIT ROCK

LOCATION Scottsdale, Arizona
COMPLETION Unbuilt
BUILDING AREA 8,500 SQ. FT.
ELEMENTS Rammed Earth, Corten, Mild Steel, Concrete, Mahogany

DESIGNED AS A CONTEMPORARY HACIENDA, Split Rock is sited parallel to the fifteenth fairway of a Scottsdale, Arizona, golf course. The natural topography and native rock of the site, including the massive split boulder from which the project takes its name, provide enclosure for two sides of the central courtyard. The L-shaped plan of the living spaces completes enclosure on the remaining two sides. A south-facing loggia links the courtyard to the entrance area, kitchen, family room, and living room. A stair was carved into a native boulder that remains in situ, facilitating the transition from the loggia to the living room level.

The perimeter walls of the house are eighteen-inch thick stabilized rammed earth, constructed from native soils to retain and enhance the material qualities and nature remnants in the existing context. The curved profile of the roof echoes surrounding rock formations and provides the dominant defining element of the building-site composition. The curvature flares upward to a dynamic overhang that prevents drainage onto the patio. Water is channeled instead to drains in the roof that flow into open cisterns that have been cut into patio paving. For privacy and solar control, all patio areas are screened by freestanding walls pierced with irregularly placed openings that frame vignettes of the Sonoran desert landscape and that contribute sculptural qualities of their own.

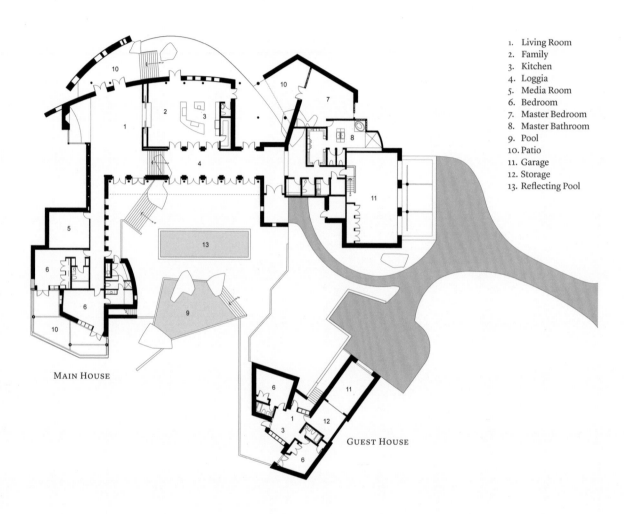

1. Living Room
2. Family
3. Kitchen
4. Loggia
5. Media Room
6. Bedroom
7. Master Bedroom
8. Master Bathroom
9. Pool
10. Patio
11. Garage
12. Storage
13. Reflecting Pool

MAIN HOUSE

GUEST HOUSE

FLOOR PLAN

EHA FAMILY TRUST

LOCATION   Wilson, Wyoming
COMPLETION   January 2010
BUILDING AREA   3,988 SQ. FT. (House); 3,346 SQ. FT. (Barn);
635 SQ. FT. (Guest House)
ELEMENTS   Reclaimed Wood, Zinc, Stone, Concrete, Corten,
Water, Cast Glass

THE SETTING FOR THIS RESIDENCE and guesthouse is a land parcel originally homesteaded by one of Jackson Hole's earliest permanent settlers. Referencing that history in the architecture and in the planning and development of the building site pays homage to the local vernacular and context, and informed the design of the buildings and the landscape. Accomplished using a palette of rustic building materials that includes shale quarried in eastern Idaho, and century-old reclaimed siding and naturally aged logs from Tensleep, Wyoming, traditional building techniques were employed in these otherwise modern, sustainable buildings. The main living areas of the single-story main house are oriented to face north, with walls of windows framing Teton views. At 3,900 square feet it is designed to be comfortable for two people, and for gracious entertaining and to accommodate more than that as well.

The traditional gambrel roof of Western barns was the source and the inspiration for the guesthouse, reinvented as a woodland beacon by the substitution of laminated glass for conventional mortar chinking. It is connected to the main house by an enclosed, transparent walkway. The siting of this relatively more vertical guesthouse gives additional definition and enclosure for an outdoor courtyard for the residence, creating a formal space within the otherwise open landscape.

W-shaped custom roof trusses provide structure and create a spatial rhythm that establishes a dynamic dialogue with the freestanding rock walls of the interior in the main house, which was designed to showcase the owner's art collection. A series of integrated water features—including four constructed ponds and a raised watercourse that is reminiscent of wooden mining flumes—invoke the home's wetland setting as the project's muse. Buildings and the reconstructed nature of the landscape fit within less than an acre of the seven-acre site, accomplished without harm to a single mature tree in the aspen grove meadow.

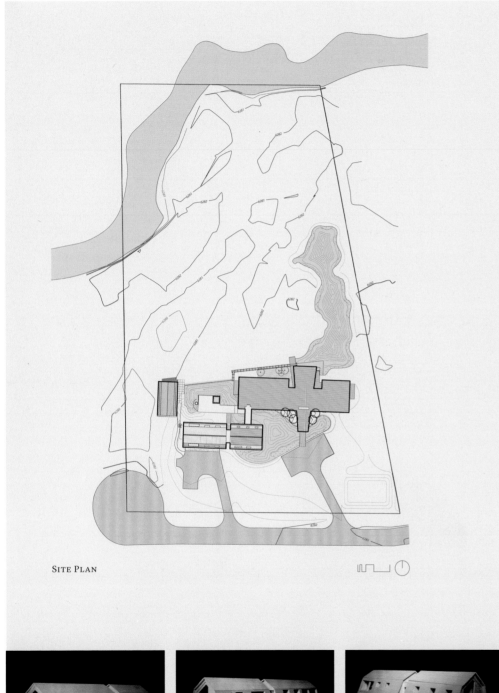

SITE PLAN

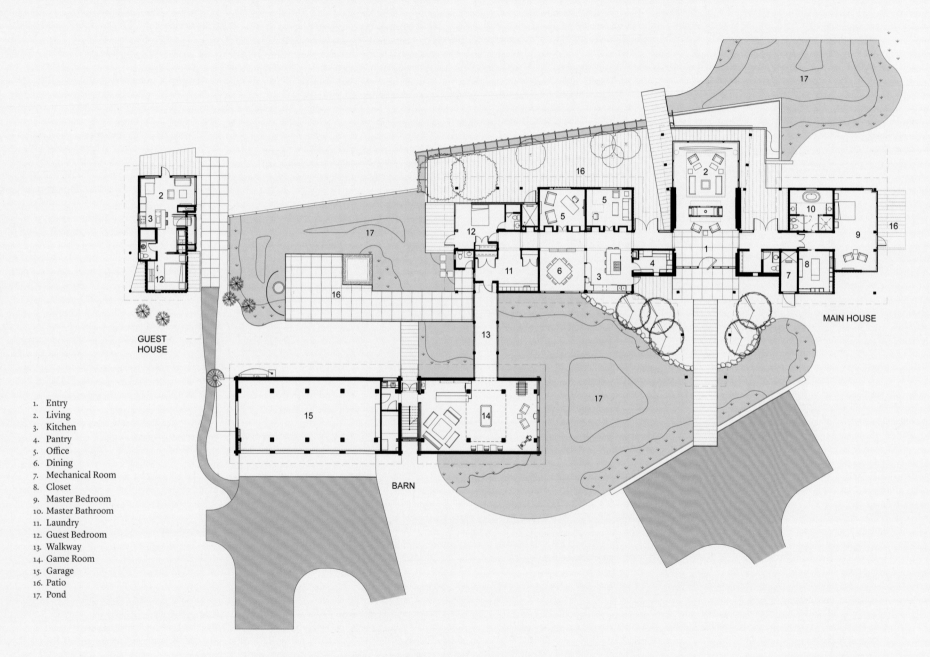

GUEST
HOUSE

MAIN HOUSE

BARN

1.   Entry
2.   Living
3.   Kitchen
4.   Pantry
5.   Office
6.   Dining
7.   Mechanical Room
8.   Closet
9.   Master Bedroom
10. Master Bathroom
11. Laundry
12. Guest Bedroom
13. Walkway
14. Game Room
15. Garage
16. Patio
17. Pond

FLOOR PLAN

TROUT RESIDENCE

LOCATION Jackson, Wyoming
COMPLETION December 2002
BUILDING AREA 5,000 SQ. FT.
ELEMENTS Sandstone, Cedar, Stained Concrete, Log, Cast Glass, Copper

THE ARCHITECTURE of the Trout residence is custom tailored to the personality of its pilot owner, with hangar-like barrel-vaulted ceilings. The house is sited and designed to provide the "airplane cockpit" view that was requested by the client. An Indiana Jones-inspired glass plank bridge with fiber-optic illumination provides access to the master suite, complementing the airplane iconography.

Sited on a long, narrow cross-ridge, the residence is fitted snugly into the land and roofed with a low-slung barrel vault to conform to strict county slope and skyline regulations. Lowering the garage into the ridge to the southwest and capping it with a native sod roof preserved the neighbor's view of Sleeping Indian Mountain, while the stone wall at the front of the garage established a datum line through the house that marks the view angle for a straight shot down the Jackson Hole airport runway in the valley below. A series of native stone walls intersect the datum wall and separate the service spaces from the main rooms of the house. The formal entry sequence passes through those stone walls, then opens to a direct view of the Grand Teton. The arched fan shape of the stairway echoes the curves of the rounded north balcony as well as the vaulted ceiling of the living room. Wood with natural finishes, the gun-blued steel that was used for the fireplace, railings and cabinetry details, and multicolored sandstone make up the array of earthy materials in this idiosyncratic residence. There are Mesoamerican influences throughout the house, another nod to the owner's passions.

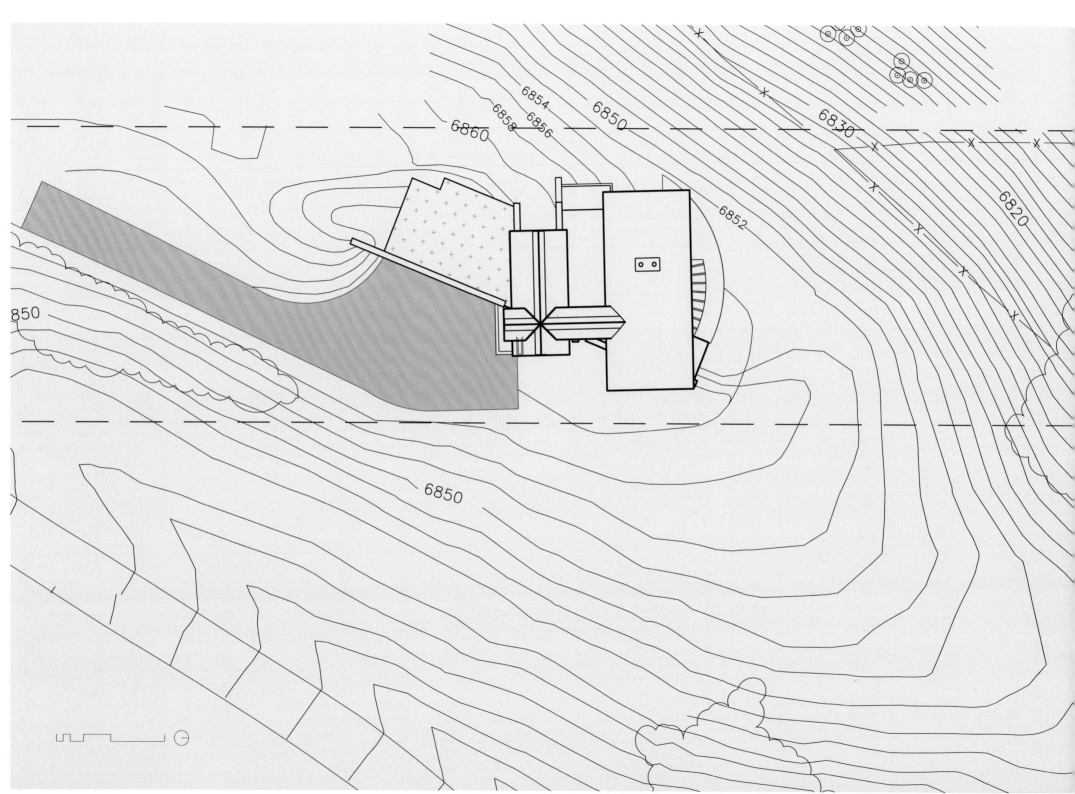

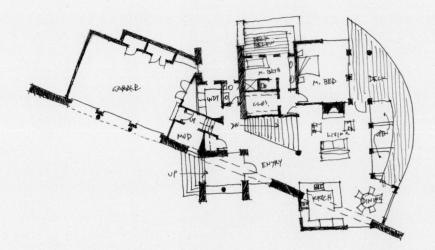

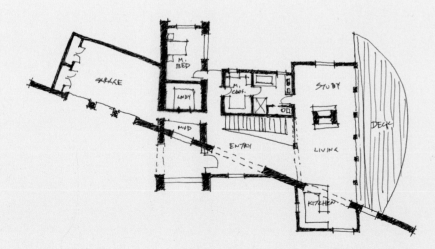

EARTH WALL II

LOCATION Squirrel, Idaho
COMPLETION July 2011
BUILDING AREA 5,994 SQ. FT.
ELEMENTS Rammed Earth, Mild Steel, Corten, Reclaimed
Wood, Reclaimed Stone, Concrete, Cedar, Maple

THE EARTH WALL II residence is as spare as its high plains setting, and literally shares the ground of its remote, 160-acre Idaho site. The use of immediately available rammed earth for walls and sod for the roof reference the historical "soddie" house type. The design of this house, a characteristic ground-scraper, evolved organically through a lengthy design-build process. It is environmentally responsive with sustainable features and palette of low-upkeep, rustic materials. A low-slope, shed roofline conforms to the horizontality of the setting while diminishing the impact of the volume and 6,000 square feet of the residence. The rammed-earth walls are post-tensioned to enhance their strength and durability in what can be a harsh climate.

Transparency is achieved on multiple levels in the design of this light-filled residence: the large glass of exterior walls opens the structure to the outdoors, and this is enhanced by continuous, poured concrete floors that seamlessly flow from patio to interior. The structure is oriented to optimize solar gain through energy efficient windows and to maximize the benefits of high-thermal mass walls. This passive solar design strategy is coupled with other green, energy-efficient features including a ground source heat pump that carries water maintained naturally at earth temperature, diminishing significantly the necessity for additional heating and cooling. Sustainable building materials also reduce environmental impacts and the home's carbon footprint: reclaimed Douglas-fir is used for soffits and sloped ceilings; reclaimed stone is used for fireplaces and chimneys; and cedar siding and fascia are treated to allow them to weather naturally. With its deliberate simplicity of design, and by incorporating materials that are site-sensitive and that will age gracefully, the house becomes an integral part of its environment, augmented by native plantings and the surrounding landscape's continually evolving character through changes of season.

1. Entry Porch
2. Entry
3. Dining
4. Living
5. Hallway
6. Office
7. Exercise Room
8. Master Suite
9. Kitchen
10. Media Room
11. Porch
12. Pantry
13. Mechanical Room
14. Sauna
15. Powder Room
16. Mudroom
17. Garage
18. Patio
19. Bedroom
20. Bunk Room Suite
21. Outdoor Shower

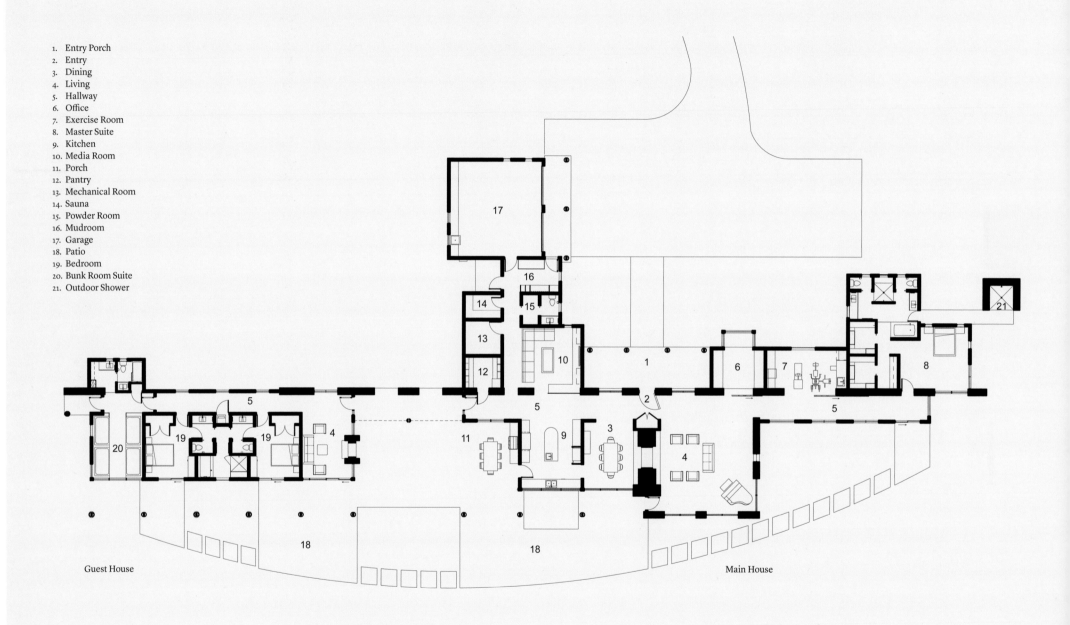

Guest House

Main House

FLOOR PLAN

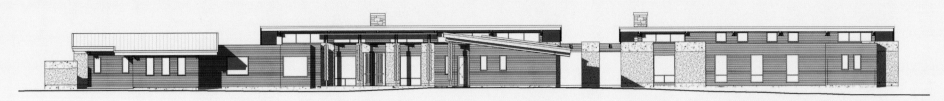

NORTH ELEVATION

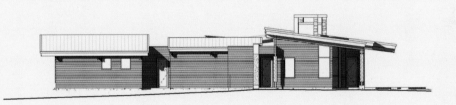

WEST ELEVATION

SOUTH ELEVATION

EAST ELEVATION

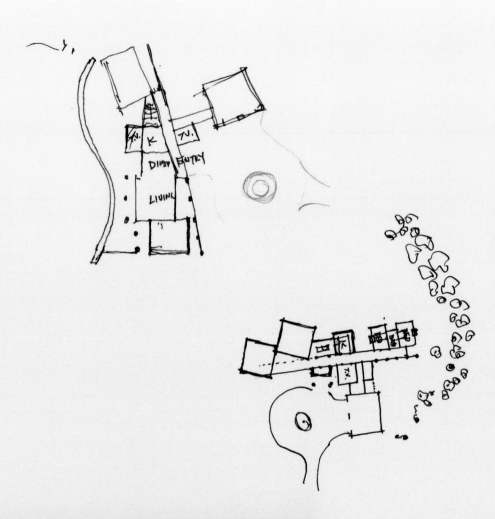

GRANITE RIDGE RESIDENCE

LOCATION Teton Village, Wyoming
COMPLETION November 2002
BUILDING AREA 5,000 SQ. FT.
ELEMENTS Log, Stone, Forged Steel, Bamboo, Glass

E FFICIENTLY ORGANIZED within an extremely tight building envelope, the two-story, foursquare scheme for the Granite Ridge residence achieves a light-filled forest aerie as proof of the architects' conviction that "a log residence can be more than a dark pile of firewood." The exterior steals some inspiration from a Tyrolean construction technique by which an apparently fortified lower floor—in this case clad in Montana shale—is topped by an overhanging upper story, here constructed of hewn and dove-tail-cut logs. The technique at once differentiates the upper public spaces from the lower and private, while offering valuable protection from high-elevation snow accumulation and the effects of the often-intense sun. A bridge between the garage and house spans a chasm that provides light and air to lower bedrooms. Finished using the same river washed stone as the residence, the chasm allows a Zen garden-like serenity into the compact site. A second-story balcony with a large dormered roof takes advantage of the home's southern exposure and captures light filtered through the tree canopy. A spa, crafted of boulders from the necessary excavation of the site, and a traditional sauna are readily accessed by way of a hydronically heated stone walk.

Four forty-foot Douglas-fir logs provide support for the steel hip trusses that define the large central space and organize the central stair in the plan, while capturing the expansiveness and feel of the forest canopy, bringing these indoors to extend the woodland aesthetic. A freestanding stair, fabricated in hand-forged stainless steel with bamboo treads, allows continuity within the interior space by never engaging the walls.

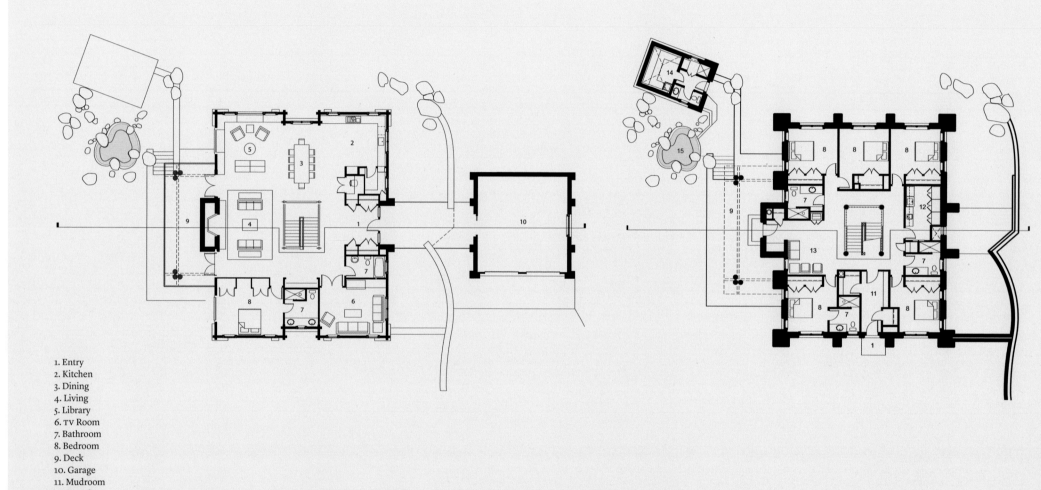

1. Entry
2. Kitchen
3. Dining
4. Living
5. Library
6. TV Room
7. Bathroom
8. Bedroom
9. Deck
10. Garage
11. Mudroom
12. Laundry
13. Sitting Area
14. Sauna
15. Hot Tub

UPPER FLOOR PLAN

LOWER FLOOR PLAN

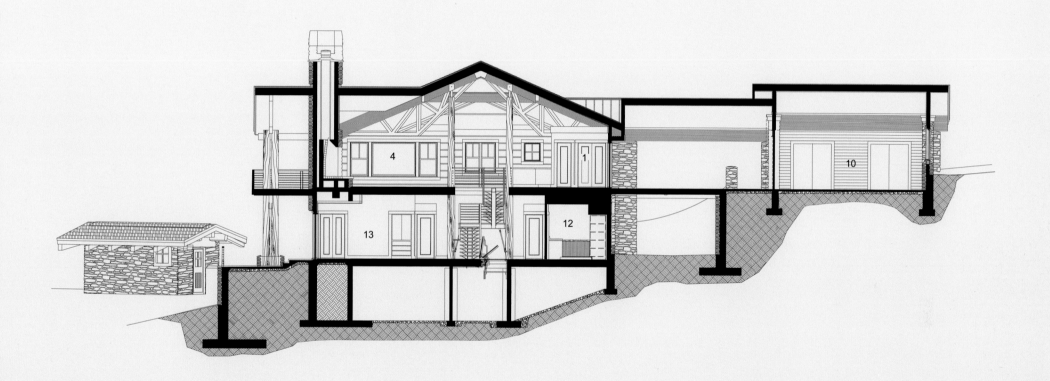

SECTION

ROSENTHAL RESIDENCE

LOCATION Wilson, Wyoming
COMPLETION November 2010
BUILDING AREA 6,773 SQ. FT.
ELEMENTS Log, Glass, Steel, Concrete

A SLEEK, ALTERNATIVE TAKE on the endemic log-home aesthetic, the Rosenthal residence recodifies traditional materials. Hand-hewn rectangular logs with dovetailed joints are used as siding, balancing the rustic aspect of the material with the precision of its application; these aspects of construction are revealed as one approaches the house. Machine-sawn, tapered Western red cedar shingles top the low-pitched shed roofs and are allowed to weather naturally. The entrance volume, intentionally compressed, opens to embrace mountains and sky. The roofline rises toward the opposite side of the house, and there a primarily glass façade thrusts outward to enhance the experience and sensation as one moves into the continuous, panoramic mountain view through the public spaces of living room, dining room and kitchen.

The floor plan is configured to take advantage of the site's raised-W landform, which runs perpendicular to the steep downward slope, using it as a device for naturally separating individual zones within the house. At the same time, as the land falls away below the decks of the home's expansive east-facing glass, there is a sense of floating above the more private lower level. To further preserve the experience of the mountain panorama, the guardrails of decks are detailed with steel flats, which make them seem to disappear. The materials selected for the interior—polished concrete floors, painted gypsum walls and wood ceilings—capture the natural light flooding the residence.

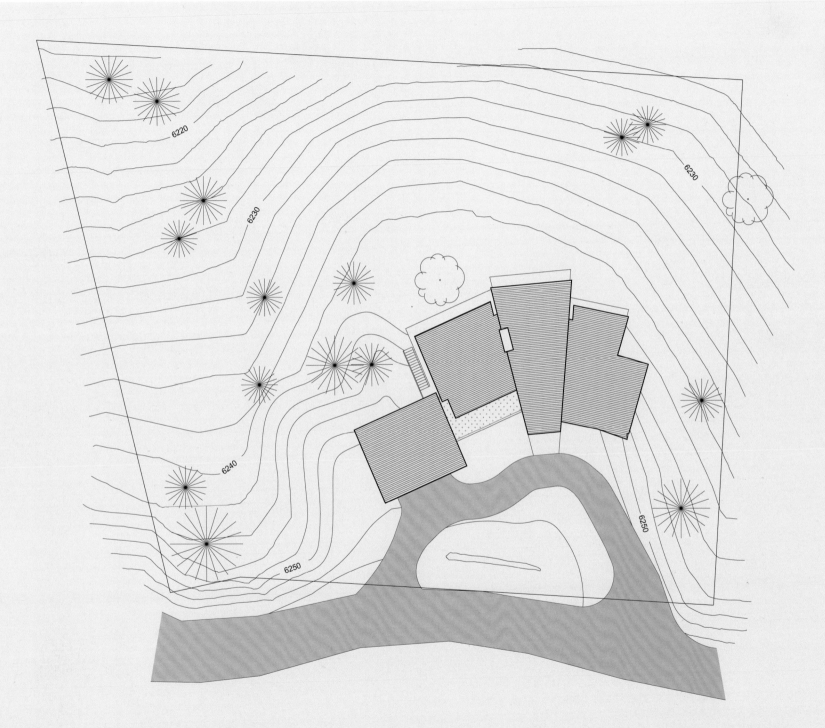

SITE PLAN

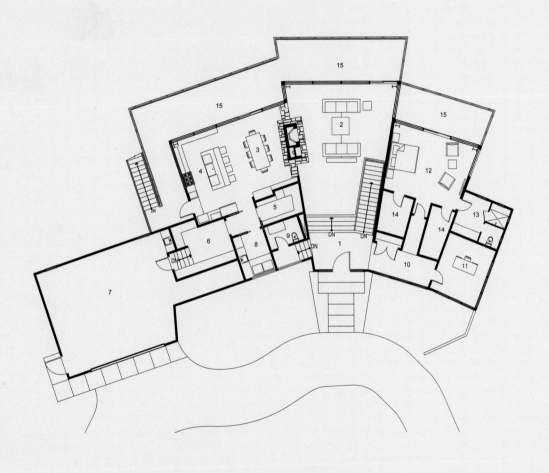

1. Entry
2. Living Area
3. Dining Room
4. Kitchen
5. Pantry
6. Mudroom
7. Garage
8. Laundry Room
9. Powder Room
10. Gallery
11. Office
12. Master Bedroom
13. Master Bathroom
14. Closet
15. Deck
16. Bedroom
17. Bathroom
18. Patio
19. Exercise Room
20. Mechanical Room
21. Storage Room

MAIN FLOOR PLAN

LOWER FLOOR PLAN

CATSKILLS RETREAT

LOCATION Livingston Manor, New York
COMPLETION Unbuilt
BUILDING AREA 285,000 SQ. FT.
ELEMENTS Bluestone, Garapa Wood, Glass, Steel, Sod

THE CATSKILLS RETREAT is located in Livingston Manor, New York. The site is at the top of a small mountain overlooking the town with distant views of Catskill National Park. The program is for a high-end resort containing 110 guest rooms, including luxury suites, tennis facilities, swimming pools, hot tubs, spa, squash courts, a bowling alley, game rooms, banquet, and conference facilities. The resort provides a variety of single family cottages and a series of outdoor trails for running, mountain biking and hiking.

Utilizing sod roofs and roof gardens the hotel fits almost seamlessly into the site reducing its visual impact in this sensitive area. The tennis facility is set into a natural embankment and bleachers are incorporated within the existing slope. A service road drops below the main porte cochere to separate public and service facilities while preserving natural views of the property. Fifty percent of the parking is placed in this service drop, which provides all of the necessary employee and valet parking and places all services, deliveries, etc. out of the public sight. Each room is oriented toward the Catskill views and has a private roof garden that doubles as the roof of the guest room or suite below. Translucent glass block skylights are incorporated into each roof garden to provide natural light into the corridors below. The design contains three distinct public nodes incorporating roof gardens and terraces for a variety of possible venues to happen simultaneously at the resort.

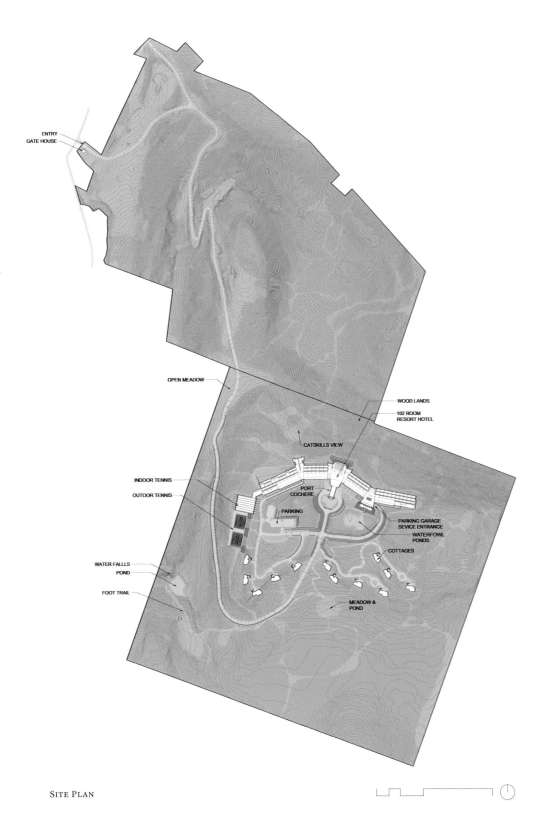

ENTRY
GATE HOUSE

OPEN MEADOW

WOOD LANDS

102 ROOM
RESORT HOTEL

CATSKILLS VIEW

INDOOR TENNIS

OUTOOR TENNIS

PORT
COCHERE

PARKING

PARKING GARAGE
SEVICE ENTRANCE

WATERFOWL
PONDS

COTTAGES

WATER FALLLS

POND

FOOT TRAIL

MEADOW &
POND

SITE PLAN

Patio
Circulation / Lobby
Roof Garden
Pool / Water Feature
Manor Deluxe
Garden Suite
Executive Suite
Presidential Suite
Reception
Spa / Recreation
Locker / Restroom
Dining
Kitchen / Service
Banquette / Meeting
Administration
Mechanical
Storage

HOTEL FLOOR PLANS
From top to bottom:
Level 0   *Spa*
Level 1   *Pool*
Level 2   *Restaurant*

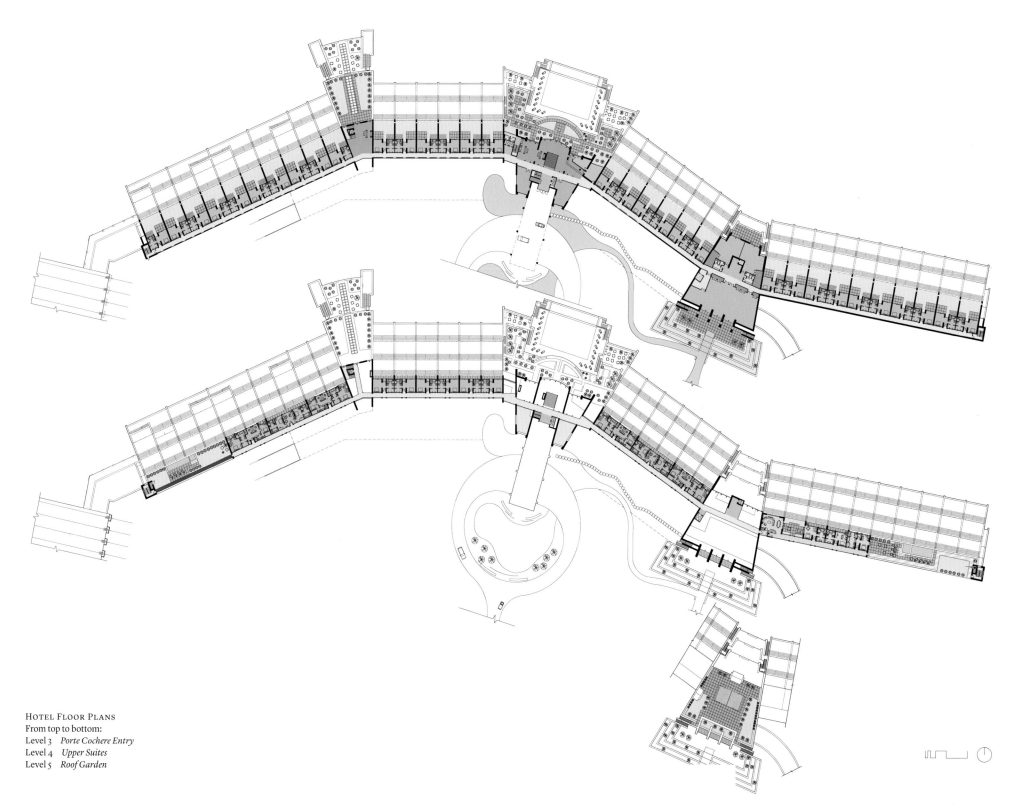

HOTEL FLOOR PLANS
From top to bottom:
Level 3   *Porte Cochere Entry*
Level 4   *Upper Suites*
Level 5   *Roof Garden*

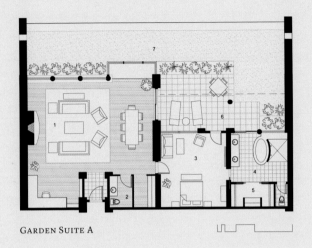

GARDEN SUITE A

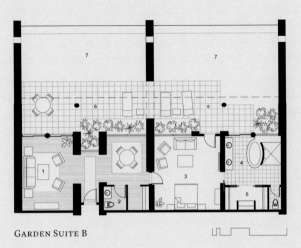

GARDEN SUITE B

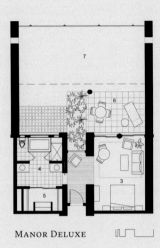

MANOR DELUXE

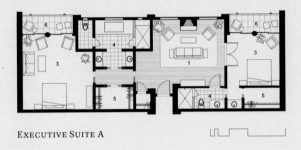

EXECUTIVE SUITE A

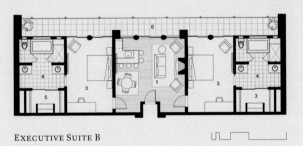

EXECUTIVE SUITE B

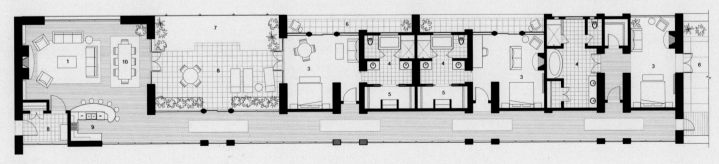

PRESIDENTIAL SUITE

1. Living Area
2. Powder Room
3. Bedroom
4. Bathroom
5. Closet
6. View Terrace
7. Roof Garden
8. Foyer
9. Kitchen
10. Dining Area

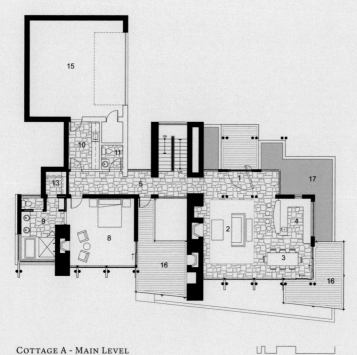

COTTAGE A - MAIN LEVEL

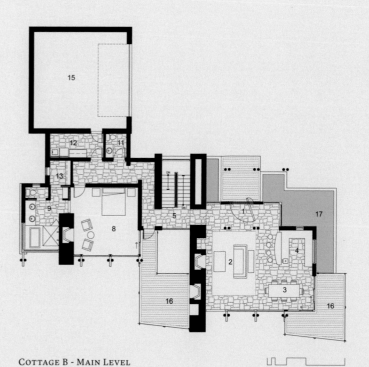

1. Entry
2. Living
3. Dining
4. Kitchen
5. Gallery
6. Bedroom
7. Bathroom
8. Master Bedroom
9. Master Bathroom
11. Powder Room
12. Mud Room
13. Closet
14. Study
15. Garage
16. Terrace
17. Reflecting Pool
18. Pool

COTTAGE B - MAIN LEVEL

COTTAGE A - LOWER LEVEL

WATERFALL

APPENDIX

WARD + BLAKE ARCHITECTS

Tom Ward & Mitch Blake

Tom Ward AIA
Mitch Blake AIA, LEED A/P
Lauralie Blake
Ken Mahood AIA
Steve Kaness
Gretchen Manning ASID
Jim Barlow AIA
SaraLee Lanier AIA
Katherine Wilson LEED A/P BD+C
Chris Jaubert AIA
Trey Terral
Brett Bennett LEED A/P BD+C
Colin Delano

PROJECT CREDITS

Green Knoll Residence
Client: Private
Project Team: Tom Ward AIA, Steve Kaness, Pegg Olson, Chris Jaubert AIA, Mark Decker, Brett Bennett, Katie Wilson, SaraLee Lanier AIA, Martina Bello
Contractor: Cox Construction
Structural Engineer: Nishkian Monks
MEP Engineer: Beaudin/ Ganze Consulting Engineers
Landscape Architect: Teton Landscape Specialties/ Agrostis, Inc.
Interior Designers: e.k. Reedy Interiors/ Lichten Craig Architects
Photographer: Paul Warchol

Landes Residence
Client: David Landes and Karen Oatey
Project Team: Mitch Blake AIA, Jim Barlow AIA, SaraLee Lanier AIA, Pegg Olson, Ken Mahood AIA
Contractor: Continental Construction
Structural Engineer: Niskian Monks
MEP Engineer: Beaudin/ Ganze Consulting Engineers
Landscape Architect: Rendezvous Engineering
Photographer: Roger Wade

Warshaw Residence
Client: Peter and Karen Warshaw
Project Team: Tom Ward AIA, Ken Mahood AIA, Ted Zimmerman AIA, SaraLee Lanier AIA, Pegg Olson, Emily McChesney
Contractor: Cox Construction
Structural Engineer: Nelson Engineering
MEP Engineer: CN Engineering
Landscape Architect: Weaver & Associates
Interior Designer: e.k. Reedy Interiors
Photographer: Douglas Kahn

TK Pad
Client: Tom Ward and Kathy Reedy
Project Team: Tom Ward AIA, Steve Kaness, SaraLee Lanier AIA, Pegg Olson
Contractor: Cox Construction
Rammed Earth Contractor: Pitzer Concrete
Structural Engineer: Niskian Monks
MEP Engineer: Boulder Engineering
Landscape Design: Tom Ward/ Teton Landscape Specialties
Interior Designer: e.k. Reedy Interiors
Photographers: Douglas Kahn, Paul Warchol, J.K. Lawrence

Day Residence
Client: Tim and Sandy Day
Project Team: Tom Ward AIA, Mitch Blake AIA, Ken Mahood AIA, Ted Zimmerman AIA, Steve Kaness
Contractor: Cox Construction
Structural Engineer: Nelson Engineering
MEP Engineer: CN Engineers
Landscape Architect: Wirth Design Associates
Interior Designer: e.k. Reedy Interiors
Photographer: Roger Wade

Villa di Famiglia Vita
Client: Mitch and Lauralie Blake
Project Team: Mitch Blake AIA, Pegg Olson, Gretchen Manning ASID, SaraLee Lanier AIA
Contractor: Headwaters Construction Company
Structural Engineer: G&S Structural Engineers
MEP Engineer: Boulder Engineering
Interior Designer: e.k. Reedy Interiors
Photographer: Roger Wade

Spring Creek Ranch
Client: Spring Creek Ranch Management Company
Project Team: Mitch Blake AIA, Tom Ward AIA, Steve Kaness, SaraLee Lanier AIA, Meghan Clements
Contractor: Jacobsen Construction
Structural Engineer: G&S Structural Engineers
MEP Engineer: Boulder Engineering
Landscape Architect: Verdone Landscape Architects
Photographer: Woolley Bugger Studios – Lark Smoothermon

Wyoming Chapter of The Nature Conservancy
Client: Gloria and Bill Newton for the Wyoming Chapter of The Nature Conservancy
Project Team: Tom Ward AIA, Bob Carter AIA, Ted Zimmerman
Contractor: Teton Heritage Builders
Rammed Earth Contractor: Jug Branjord
Structural Engineer: Nelson Engineering
Photographer: Douglas Kahn

Teton County Children's Learning Center, "The Ranch"
(Collaboration with D.W. Arthur & Associates Architects)
Client: Teton County Wyoming
Collaborating Architect: Woody Arthur AIA, Kelly Ryan AIA
Project Team: Mitch Blake AIA, Tom Ward AIA, Ken Mahood AIA, Chris Jaubert AIA, Mallory Martin, Trey Terrell, Katie Wilson, Dan Amborski
Contractor: Headwaters Construction Company
Structural Engineer: Pillar Structural Engineering
MEP Engineer: Beaudin/ Ganze Consulting Engineers
Civil Engineering: Jorgensen Associates
Landscape Architect: Herschberger Design
Children's Playgrounds: Lori Ryker – Artemis Institute/ Remote Studio
Photographer: Roger Wade

PLC Residence

Client: Private

Project Team: Mitch Blake AIA, Jim Barlow AIA, SaraLee Lanier AIA, Trey Terrell, Pegg Olson, Dan Amborski

Renderings: Trey Terrell

Structural Engineer: G&S Structural Engineers

Mechanical Engineer: CN Engineering

Landscape Architect: Weaver & Associates

Three Creek Residence

Client: Private

Project Team: Tom Ward AIA, SaraLee Lanier AIA, Brett Bennett, Chris Jaubert AIA

Renderings: SaraLee Lanier AIA

Sharp Residence

Client: David and Lisa Sharp

Project Team: Mitch Blake AIA, SaraLee Lanier AIA, Trey Terrell

Renderings: SaraLee Lanier AIA

Split Rock

Client: Gloria and Bill Newton

Project Team: Tom Ward AIA, Bob Carter AIA, Ted Zimmerman AIA

Structural Engineering: Verde Valley Engineering

EHA Residence

Client: Private

Project Team: Tom Ward AIA, Jim Barlow AIA, Gretchen Manning ASID, SaraLee Lanier AIA, Katie Wilson, Mark Decker, Chris Jaubert AIA, Trey Terrell, Brett Bennett, Mallory Martin

Contractor: Tom Stoner Construction

Structural Engineer: Pillar Structural Engineering

MEP Engineer: Van Boerum & Frank Associates

Landscape Architect: Verdone Landscape Architects

Interior Designer: e.k. Reedy Interiors

Photographer: Roger Wade, David Swift

Trout Residence

Client: Everett and Sandra Trout

Project Team: Mitch Blake AIA, Bob Carter AIA, Gretchen Manning ASID, Ted Zimmerman AIA, Steve Kaness

Contractor: Bancroft Construction

Structural Engineer: Nelson Engineering

MEP Engineer: CN Engineering

Landscape Designer: Rhon McKee

Interior Designers: Susan Okamoto Interiors/ The Red Chair

Photographer: Douglas Kahn

Earth Wall II

Client: Private

Project Team: Mitch Blake AIA, Jim Barlow AIA, SaraLee Lanier AIA, Trey Terrell, Katie Wilson, Pegg Olson, Brett Bennett

Contractor: Headwaters Construction

Rammed Earth Contractor: StrongCrete

Structural Engineer: McNeil Group

MEP Engineer: ES2 Engineering System Solutions

Landscape Architect: David Weaver & Associates

Interior Designer: e.k. Reedy Interiors

Photographer: Roger Wade

Granite Ridge Residence

Client: Private

Project Team: Tom Ward AIA, Jim Barlow AIA, Steve Kaness, Gretchen Manning ASID, SaraLee Lanier AIA

Contractor: Jim Roscoe Construction

Structural Engineer: Nelson Engineering

MEP Engineer: Boulder Engineering

Landscape Architect: Wirth Design Associates

Interior Designer: e.k. Reedy Interiors

Photographer: Douglas Kahn

Rosenthal Residence

Client: Private

Project Team: Tom Ward AIA, Steve Kaness, Pegg Olson, Gretchen Manning ASID, Katie Wilson, Trey Terral, Brett Bennett

Contractor: Cox Construction

Structural Engineer: McNeil Group

MEP Engineer: CN Engineering

Landscape Architect: Naturescape Designs

Interior Designer: e.k. Reedy Interiors

Photographer: Roger Wade

Catskills Retreat

Client: Private

Project Team: Mitch Blake AIA, Tom Ward AIA, Jim Barlow AIA, SaraLee Lanier AIA, Trey Terrell, Katie Wilson, Brett Bennett

Renderings: Pacificon Multimedia, LLC

Additional Photography Credits

The historical images on pages 7, 8, 13, 14, and 260 were generously donated by the Jackson Hole Historical Society and Museum.

Landscape photography on project title pages by Ed Riddell: pages 2, 22, 54, 74, 90, 100, 118, 150, 176, 194, 208, 226, 244, and 267

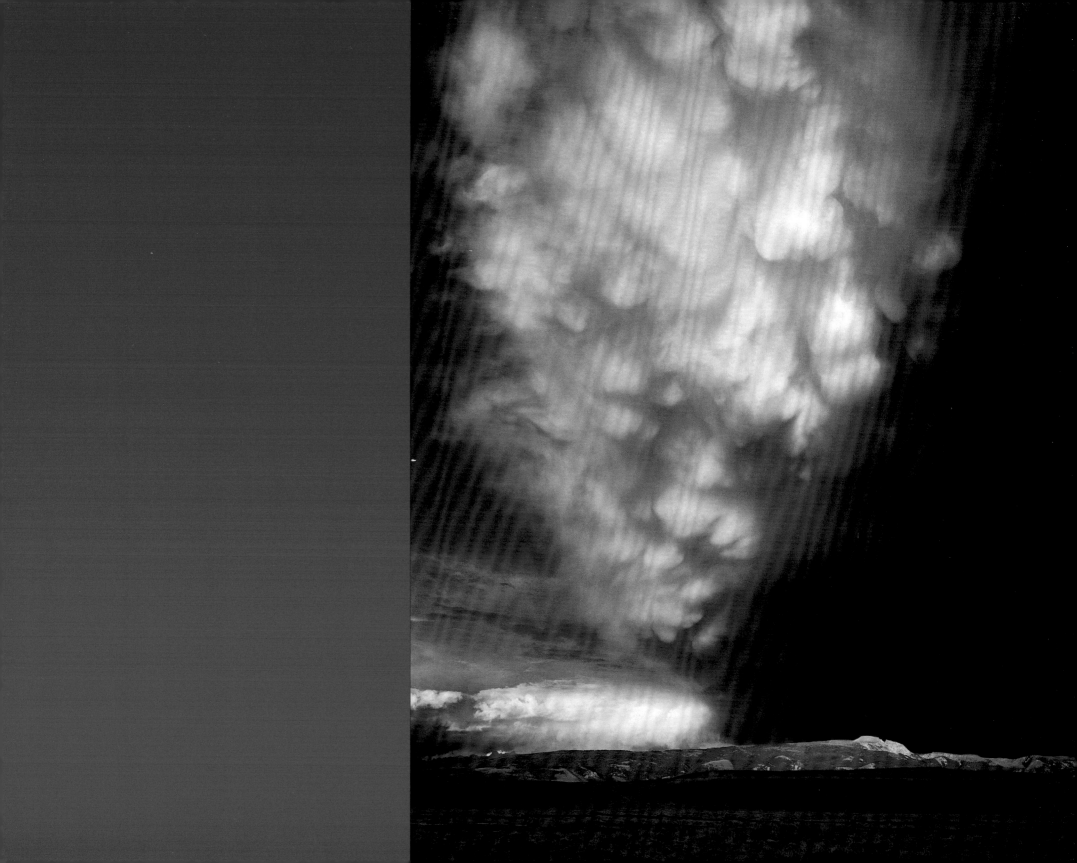

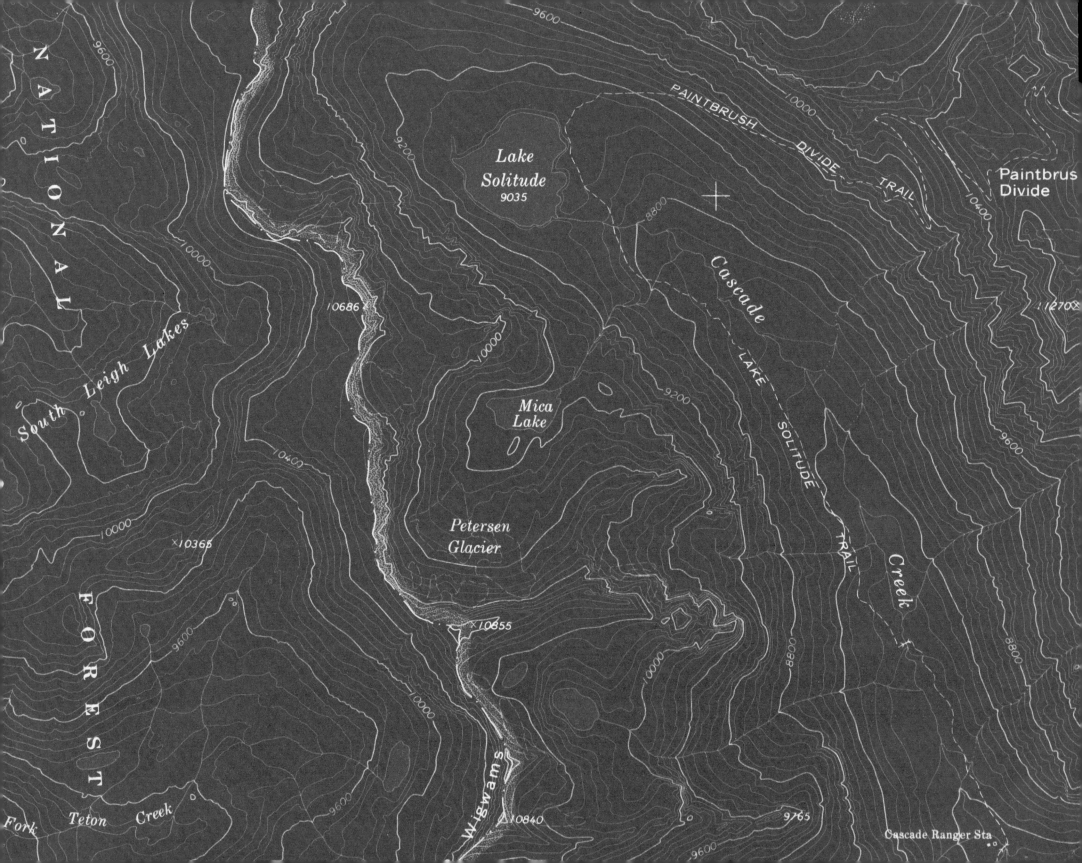